Using Drama to Teach
Personal, Social and
Emotional Skills

A Lucky Duck Book

Using Drama to Teach Personal, Social and Emotional Skills

Jacqui O'Hanlon and Angie Wootten

P·C·P

Paul Chapman
Publishing

Paul Chapman Publishing
A SAGE Publications Company
1 Oliver's Yard
55 City Road
London EC1Y 1SP

SAGE Publications Inc.
2455 Teller Road
Thousand Oaks, California 91320

SAGE Publications India Pvt Ltd
B 1/I1 Mohan Cooperative Industrial Area
Mathura Road, Post Bag 7
New Delhi 110 044

SAGE Publications Asia-Pacific Pte Ltd
33 Pekin Street #02-01
Far East Square
Singapore 048763

www.luckyduck.co.uk

Commissioning editors: George Robinson and Barbara Maines
Editorial team: Mel Maines, Sarah Lynch, Wendy Ogden
Illustrator: Philippa Drakeford

Library of Congress Control Number 2007921441

British Library Cataloguing in Publication data

A catalogue record for this book is available from the British Library

ISBN 978 1 4129 1821 3

Typeset by C & M Digitals, Chennai, India
Printed in India by Replika Press, India
Printed on paper from sustainable resources

Contents

Acknowledgements

We are very grateful to the British Association of Teachers of the Deaf which awarded us a scholarship from the Mary Grace Wilkins Travel Fund to trial the materials within this book with teachers of the deaf and deaf children in the UK. We are also grateful for the organisation's support and encouragement with the project, giving opportunities for us to give workshops and promote the materials with teachers of the deaf.

We gratefully acknowledge the contribution of West Midlands Quaker Peace Education Project (WMQPEP). Some of these materials were first created for their school-based programme. Other exercises are drawn from their existing materials and are used with their kind permission.

We would like to thank Dr Stephen Powers and Dr Linda Watson who run Birmingham University's course for training teachers of the deaf. They have supported and encouraged us by providing workshop opportunities to promote drama to trainee teachers of the deaf, thereby allowing more materials to be trialled and more interest to be generated.

For trialling our materials we are indebted to teachers Jo Butler and the children of Peterbrook Primary School Resource Base in Shirley; Jane Bishop and the children of Benton Park Primary School Resource Base in Newcastle-upon-Tyne; and Sarah Miller and the children of the Willingdon Primary School Hearing Support Facility in Eastbourne. Thank you to the teachers who gave us valuable feedback.

Angie would like to thank the service co-ordinator of the Hearing Advisory Team in Warwickshire, Viv Pierce-Jones, for her support in giving time for the book to be researched and written. Thanks, too, to the wider Warwickshire management team for support given.

We thank Mike and Ellen Ross at Grove House, Bromesberrow Heath near Ledbury for providing us with a tranquil hideaway to begin and end the writing of this book.

Overwhelmingly we would like to thank our families and friends for their support and encouragement. In particular, Angie would like to thank her husband David for his encouragement, patience and advice.

To all of you, we thank you.

How to Use the CD-ROM

The CD-ROM contains PDF files, labelled 'Activity Sheets.pdf' which consist of worksheets for each lesson in this resource. You will need Acrobat Reader version 3 or higher to view and print these resources.

The documents are set up to print to A4 but you can enlarge them to A3 by increasing the output percentage at the point of printing using the page set-up settings for your printer.

To photocopy the worksheets directly from this book, set your photocopier to enlarge by 125% and align the edge of the page to be copied against the leading edge of the copier glass (usually indicated by an arrow).

Introduction

Who is this book for?

There is a very good reason why this handbook is useful for teachers involved with a broad range of children. In this book we promote the use of drama, and in so doing draw on and channel the innate sense of play in almost every child. Most children like to play and, consequently, many of them respond positively to taking part in drama.

In fact this handbook has been written with a certain group of children in mind – deaf children (the term 'deaf' is used to denote all children who have a degree of hearing impairment). However, as teachers of the deaf are constantly saying, 'Good practice with deaf children is good practice for all'. Consequently we envisage that this handbook will be useful for normally hearing children. It will have an application for children with communication difficulties, including children on the autistic spectrum. It will also have relevance for older children with learning difficulties. Finally, it will be useful for mixed groups of children, for example deaf and hearing children in a mainstream setting.

Clearly all groups of children are different and each teacher will know the needs of a particular group. However, we imagine that the resources will be most applicable to a primary or early secondary environment.

Children and personal, social and emotional skills

All children, including deaf children, have personal, social and emotional needs. Goleman (1996), in his influential book *Emotional Intelligence,* promotes this stance, and Moseley (1993) states that enhancing self-esteem in children is the most important task that schools have to face.

The importance of these needs is reflected within the National Curriculum, with its non-statutory guidelines for Personal, Social and Health Education (PSHE). In the introductory section, 'The school curriculum and the National Curriculum: values, aims and purposes', the development of skills to deal with these needs are advocated. The reasons for this are twofold; these skills form a preparation for life, and have a significant part to play in a youngster's ability to learn and achieve (DfEE/QCA, 1999). The instinct that such skills are paramount for children has crystallised into the Department for Education and Skills' (DfES) initiative: social and emotional aspects of learning (SEAL). A quick glance at the main aspects chosen for promotion by the DfES – self-awareness, managing feelings, motivation, empathy and social skills – will show a happy correlation with the skills on which we have chosen to concentrate within this handbook. Consequently, it is hoped that this handbook will give teachers a tool for approaching the delivery of SEAL.

Deaf children and personal, social and emotional skills

Deaf children have a need to develop PSHE skills as much as any other children. Some would say they have a greater need since deafness may create a barrier to developing these crucial life-enhancing skills. There are a number of reasons as to why this need arises. First, there is the possible disruption in the mother–baby bond created by the diagnosis of deafness in the child (Luterman, 1987; Marschark, 1993) with ensuing effects on language and communication (Webster and Wood, 1989). Deaf children may receive less explanation from their parents about feelings than hearing children (Gregory, 1976). Delayed language development in deaf children may mean that their vocabulary does not extend to cover everything they feel. They lack a vocabulary to describe their emotions and could therefore be described as being less 'emotionally literate' than other children. Because of the communication barrier, deaf children may not have the same opportunities to know that other people have the same, and different, feelings and aspirations as themselves. Because they are less aware of this range of feelings in others, they may not always respond appropriately. This type of awareness and response is usually summed up in the word 'empathy'. Deaf children may be less empathetic than others. Because of lack of experience they may find it more difficult to respond to social cues (Moore et al., 1999). Some deaf children may have poorer self-esteem than hearing children (Bat-Chava, 1993). They may have more difficulty making and sustaining friendships and, as a result, experience social isolation (Moore et al., 1999).

Most practitioners involved with deaf children will recognise how such traits are manifest. It may be the unresolved squabbles on the playground that linger on into lessons, disrupting learning. Perhaps it is a child's apparent inability to accept himself as deaf which in turn disrupts his ability to assert his needs. It may be a child's inability to express how she feels. Thus, in our experience, targets on the Individual Education Plan (IEP) of a deaf child that pinpoint PSHE skills are as common as those relating to language development or any area of the curriculum. Often the question for a practitioner is how to deal with such targets, and in this handbook we hope to offer some answers.

What is the background to using drama with children with special needs, including deaf children?

For several decades, drama has been seen as a valuable tool in the education of children with special needs. Dorothy Heathcote, a leading drama practitioner working from the 1950s onwards and widely respected for her contribution of bringing drama into schools, was also well-known for her drama work with 'handicapped' children. In 1979 the report of the Warnock Committee endorsed the use of drama as having an important place in the education of children with special needs (Warnock, 1978), and since then there have been many other advocates.

We have already drawn attention to the fact that drama uses an innate sense that almost all children, including deaf children, naturally have: that of play. Play is the way in which children learn for themselves. The importance of play in education has been very well documented, with Piaget probably being the best known proponent. When play is channelled and structured in the drama lesson it can become a vital tool for learning.

Drama involves the use of the body, including the face. Children learn by *doing* rather than, primarily, by listening or communicating. Action rather than speech lies at the heart of drama. In fact, drama can be a virtually non-verbal means of learning, while mime and gesture can be enhanced. Thus, drama can be a crucial and accessible form of self-expression for some deaf children.

However, conversely, we can also say that drama provides rich opportunities for the development of language. The advantage is that language is generated organically from the drama situation rather than being imposed. Thus language arising is natural and relevant.

These unique attributes of drama have been recognised by practitioners involved with deaf children for some time now (Cayton, 1981; Seeley and Camus, 1983; Powers et al., 1999). They can also be seen as being wholly relevant to children with language and communication issues, in general.

Why then might drama be particularly useful in the development of PSHE skills?

Of itself, the process of drama is an exercise in social interaction. There is the choice of roles, the entering into a group activity, and the co-operation and engagement with other children. Set up in the way we advocate in this handbook, children are involved in agreeing the 'rules' for co-operation in the drama experience before they start.

In drama a child can try out new roles and therefore have new opportunities to be and to feel. It is a unique chance to 'put oneself in someone else's shoes' – to feel as they feel. For deaf children this may be an important opportunity as chances to learn vicariously about the feelings of others may not occur.

We have already spoken of the non-verbal nature of drama. The accurate reading of non-verbal cues such as gestures, facial expressions and mime are key to understanding each other's feelings. Drama gives an important opportunity to hone these skills of expression and interpretation, the better to recognise these emotions in others.

In drama children can be invited to respond personally to a range of social scenarios. With these opportunities comes the possibility of responding in different ways with an invitation to consider which, given the consequences, might be more appropriate. Within these situations children can be encouraged to show how they feel and to link these facial and body expressions to the language of emotional literacy.

Is the drama we are proposing different from that for hearing children?

We have used best and current drama practice as the backbone of the modules in this handbook. Many of the ideas behind the exercises and games are well known and well tried by drama practitioners involved in mainstream practice. They have been used extensively by the authors in working with children with poor self-esteem and are arranged and modified here to suit our aims. Completely new material has also been created to meet our objectives.

The modules described in the next pages differ from standard programmes for normally hearing children in four key respects:

- core content
- language
- amount of content
- position.

Core content
The content of the programmes has been designed to deal specifically with issues which sometimes affect deaf children but which, as we have said, may well affect other children as well. These are:

- being able to identify feelings and label them (emotional literacy)
- being able to recognise these feelings in others (empathy)

- being able to make friends
- being able to keep friends (conflict resolution)
- being happy with who they are (self-esteem)
- being able to be proactive about needs (assertiveness and confidence).

Language content

It is recognised that the language of deaf children is sometimes delayed. Therefore, the language of games and exercises has been adapted in an attempt to suit need. (See the next section 'Using this Book' for further details about this aspect.) Clearly practitioners may be speaking and/or signing with children.

Amount of content

We believe that the best drama lessons are kept pacey and dynamic, with children learning by doing rather than by listening or, in the case of signing children, watching explanation. However, we recognise that sometimes more explanation will be needed, more visual clues will need to be incorporated and more modelling and demonstrating might be needed than for hearing children. Consequently, we have tailored the content of each lesson appropriately, keeping aims clear and simple.

Positions

The need that deaf children have to lip-read or watch signs is crucial. Thus, the main speaker must be clearly visible all the time. This has implications for some games and activities. The configuration for seating or standing has been engineered to meet this need, for example games where the main speaker is standing in a circle have been changed to a semicircle shape where the speaker now stands where he or she can be seen by all. Clearly, if you are not involved with deaf children, games that are described as being played 'in a semicircle' can be played in a circle.

Using this Book

In this section the content and structure of the handbook are described, as well as how to use the book.

Content

The personal, social and emotional aspects dealt with are represented by six modules entitled:

> 'I Can Express How I Feel'
> 'I Know How You Feel'
> 'I Can Make Friends'
> 'I Can Keep Friends'
> 'I'm Happy Being Me'
> 'I Can Express What I Need'.

Each module begins with a description of the aims relating to it.

Structure

There are three to five sessions within each module. At the start of the session there is an 'Objectives' section outlining the objectives for the particular session. This is followed by a 'Materials and preparation' section in which the resources needed for the session are explained. Many of these resources are available on the CD-ROM. Although resources are provided, you may like to create your own resources based on the precise needs of the group of children you teach. For instance this may mean that you want to draw on incidents that have really happened to members of the group to create scenarios for the group drama work. To do this will give the drama work an immediacy and a relevance to the children.

Within the section, 'Materials and preparation', it is made clear for which game or exercise of the session each resource is to be prepared.

Within the first modules there are ideas within the 'Materials and preparation' sections for creating random pairings or groups, for example, cutting up birthday cards into fours, giving each child a piece and asking all the children to find children with the corresponding pieces of their cards. These are suggestions that may be followed to create variety and interest.

Each session follows a shape made up of the following elements:

- games
- core activities
- reflection on the drama
- closing games.

Here are some notes on each of these elements.

Games (including closing games)

We have used a number of different types of drama games within the structure of the programmes. Apart from being fun, these different types of games have different purposes. The different types of games and a short description of their purpose follows. It will be noted that the purpose behind some of the games is actually to build social skills. It will also be noticed that within the modules some games come under more than one category of game.

Introductory name games These games are designed to give children the chance to acknowledge each other and, in some cases, to learn new names. Through their content they may also reinforce a skill explored in the previous session. Alternatively they may introduce a new skill to be developed within the session.

Mixing-up games Children often like to sit next to other children they know. However, we want to encourage children to work with children they don't know so well. This is a way of moving children out of their 'comfort zones'.

Affirmation games These games are designed to encourage children to show that they value each other. In the games they show this by repeating back what another member of the group has said or done. These games are also often known as 'name games'.

Co-operative group games These are games based on developing co-operative skills and a sense of group achievement among the children.

End activities and end games These activities are designed to 'finish off' the sessions. They may reinforce what the children have been learning in the sessions, they may affirm the group – or just be pure fun!

We are mindful that it may take more time and more modelling to teach deaf children new games than it takes for normally hearing children. However, we would encourage you to persevere as the results are often well worth it!

Core activities

These activities involve the children in drama exercises designed to form the centre of the learning experience for each session. They are key to the progression of the module.

Reflection on the drama

After some exercises, especially after the core activities, there is a section called 'Process'. This is an opportunity for the pupils to reflect. In some instances they are encouraged to reflect on the skills they have needed to play the games effectively. By talking about these skills, the rules of successful co-operation in drama are drawn out from the children themselves. In other instances it may be that the children enter into a reflective discussion about what the drama exercise they have been engaged in has shown them about the particular theme being dealt with in the module. This in turn will help them to advance their understanding and experience of the skills being developed.

Adaptations to the materials

We are conscious of the fact that the children you teach, whether deaf or not, are individuals, with individual needs. Consequently, you will want to tailor your lessons to the needs of individual pupils. You may also have constraints within the environment in which you are working, for example, space or time.

We have taken into consideration that you may wish to make changes in the games that you use. In some cases it is possible to interchange one game for another. We have included a 'Compendium of Games' at the end of this book so that, if you feel that a certain game is unsuitable for the children you teach, you may choose another from the corresponding category of game. This may be particularly necessary if children are deaf and signing.

Exercises are less interchangeable, although within some modules suggestions have been made for possible alternatives.

Communication Modes

Whilst writing this book we have been mindful of a possible range of different communication modes used by both teacher and child within the drama sessions we have described. Depending on the child – whether deaf or, for a variety of reasons, having communication difficulties – he or she may be employing speech or some type of sign language, or indeed using both. In turn you as teachers may be using a range of communication modes. In many instances within this book we have been able to reflect and honour this range, employed by both children and teachers, by using words such as 'communicate' and 'express'. However, in some instances we have needed to use the phrase 'sign or say' or variations of it. We acknowledge that the most correct form is 'sign and/or say' but, for ease of reading, have chosen the form 'sign or say'. Therefore it should be assumed that the phrase 'sign or say' denotes using any appropriate mode of communication.

Assessment and evaluation

We recognise that it is vital to establish the efficacy of the modules as far as the children's development is concerned. To do this one must be clear about the achievements of the children before the modules are embarked upon. From there it will be possible to mark success for each child. We have included an 'Assessment and Evaluation' sheet on the accompanying CD-ROM which teachers may find helpful in assessing 'where individual children are' before a module is embarked upon, and again after the module is completed.

We suggest that, in the first instance, progression for a child will relate to how he or she responds to exercises within the module. For example, in a particular exercise a child may respond to a scenario in such a way as to suggest that he or she understands another child's feeling and is able to react appropriately to it within the drama. This is where an assistant may be extremely valuable in noting down observations of the children that may afterwards be used to form a judgement as to the child's progress.

Clearly, teachers will also be interested in the more long-term effect of the modules on the children's skills. To facilitate this we have included pointers for teachers to encourage the transfer of new skills from the drama sessions into wider environments. Thus, for example, in Module Six, 'I Can

Express What I Need', we suggest a collaboration with mainstream teachers in praising and encouraging children who, after the module, are able to be more proactive about their needs in a mainstream class.

Other practical issues

Progression between modules

Ideally the modules in this book should be used on a regular basis and as a continuous curriculum. We also suggest that they are used in the sequence given in the book. There is a direct progression between some of the modules – for instance, between the first module, 'I Can Express How I Feel', and the second module, 'I Know How You Feel'. The third module, 'I Can Make Friends', follows on directly to the fourth module, 'I Can Keep Friends'. Similarly the fifth module, 'I'm Happy Being Me', leads into 'I Can Express What I Need'. Research has shown that a continuing, developing curriculum is more effective over time than short programmes (Goleman, 1996).

Groupings

We offer a few suggestions regarding the composition of groups. We have designed the modules in this handbook for use with groups of children. Ideally, the group size should be six or more children. In a unit or specialised school such a group, with similar needs, might be feasible. Where children with a special need are being educated individually in mainstream schools, outreach teachers may like to consider gathering youngsters together across a region for a series of sessions. Such a suggestion will have logistic implications but the potential benefits to pupils are obvious.

Using the programmes with a mixed group of children – children with a special need together with peers in the mainstream class – may be another worthwhile option. In a unit situation each child may be encouraged to bring a friend from mainstream to join them for the sessions. In this case, thought should be given as to the composition of the mainstream children in the group. One of the aims of the programmes is to build self-esteem and confidence in children. Therefore, children joining the group should be either supportive of their unit peers or have similar needs themselves, for example emotional literacy needs. Careful thought and liaison with mainstream colleagues needs to be given to the make-up of the group so that it is beneficial to all.

It is also possible to use these modules with whole classes of pupils.

The role of teaching assistants

Teaching assistants perform very important roles within these sessions. Teachers will do well to consider the most effective ways in which their teaching assistants' time may be used. These are the possible range of roles they may perform:

- modelling games and exercises with the teacher
- signing to individual children
- scribing on flipcharts
- providing additional explanation to individual children
- helping children with writing
- working with small groups helping children to create drama scenes
- observing individual children
- photographing, videoing
- taking notes based on the achievements of individual children
- sharing observations after the sessions with the teachers
- discussing IEP targets relating to the aims of the modules with the children
- facilitating the transfer of skills into other environments, for example, the mainstream class, the playground.

Two important final notes

We believe that it is important for children to be praised and for their work to be affirmed and celebrated. This creates a positive role model for the very personal and social skills we are trying to enhance in them.

Last but by no means least, it is our aim for each session that both children and staff should have fun! We hope you do!

Assessment and evaluation

Use the following rating system to assess the impact of the programme on individual pupils.

5	4	3	2	1
Excellent	Good	Satisfactory	Poor	Very poor

PUPIL NAME...

Questions	Before programme	At the end of programme	Evidence of transfer
Ability to understand vocabulary relating to emotions			
Ability to use a range of appropriate vocabulary in identifying emotions			
Ability to recognise and name own emotions			
Ability to recognise different emotions in others			
Ability to respond appropriately to different emotions in others			
Ability to show interest in others by remembering information about them			

Using Drama to Teach Personal, Social and Emotional Skills, Paul Chapman Publishing, A Lucky Duck Book © Jacqui O'Hanlon and Angie Wootten, 2007.

Questions	Before programme	At the end of programme	Evidence of transfer
Ability to share with others			
Ability to show trustworthiness			
Ability to demonstrate empathy			
Ability to avoid unnecessary confrontation			
Ability to implement strategies for dealing with anger and frustration			
Ability to affirm themselves			
Ability to affirm others			
Ability to know their own needs			
Ability to express their own needs appropriately			

Using Drama to Teach Personal, Social and Emotional Skills, Paul Chapman Publishing, A Lucky Duck Book © Jacqui O'Hanlon and Angie Wootten, 2007.

Module One
'I Can Express What I Feel'

The aims of this three-session module are twofold. First, the module introduces the children to drama as a route to developing social skills. The children play a range of games that engage them in skills of collaboration and affirmation as well as requiring them to trust each other. The second aim is to give pupils the opportunity to explore their feelings. They will consider how many different feelings we have, and how quickly feelings can change. Over the course of the sessions they will develop and extend their emotional vocabulary. They will also begin to consider situations that trigger particular emotional reactions.

Session 1: Beginnings

Objectives

- To encourage introductions between the children.
- To establish a trusting and friendly atmosphere.
- To begin to introduce a 'feelings vocabulary'.

Materials and preparation

- An interesting object – a ball, a furry animal, a precious stone (for *'Middle, left, right'*).
- Use *'Getting into pairs'* (from the CD-ROM). Print so that each child will have one piece of paper with a word on it (for *'Pairs – still images'*).
- Flipchart and pens (for *'Pairs – still images'*).

Introductory name game

Middle, left, right

The children should be sitting in a circle. Introduce a 'talking object' (when the child holds it they may talk or sign). The idea is to pass the object around the circle and each person to first introduce themselves and then the person on their left and right. Model this for the children by saying or signing, for example, 'I'm Mr Phillips, and this is Charlie and this is Ayesha'.

Mixing-up games

Walking name call

Explain that in a moment you will turn your chair out of the circle, say/sign someone's name and walk towards him or her. They will then get up so you can sit in their chair. Then they will say/sign someone else's name and walk towards them and sit in their chair, and so on around the circle until everyone's name has been called and everyone has moved seats. Each person can only be called once. Ask the group what signal they could use to show that someone has been called? (Arms folded, for example.) The last person calls the leader. Once a pattern has been established, repeat the identical pattern again, so everyone has to remember whose name they called and sit again in their seat. Repeat the same pattern two or three times each time speeding up the game.

Process Ask the children what skills they were using to play that game (or what they were doing that made the game go well). For example you are looking for words that suggest memory, concentration, helping each other if someone got stuck.

'The sun shines on . . . '
For this game the circle of chairs needs to widened to create a semicircle. Turn your chair out of the semicircle and stand in a position in front of the semicircle so that everyone can see you. The idea of this game is that everyone moves who falls into the category that you present. For example, say or sign, 'The sun shines on everyone who can ride a bike'. All the children who can ride a bike then change places with one another and you find a place as well. The new person standing has to carry on the game with their own phrase starting with 'The sun shines on . . . '.

Process Again, ask the children what makes that game work well. You may be looking for words that suggest: reacting quickly, thinking of new categories, walking across the semicircle.

Explain to the children that doing drama work means using faces and bodies to tell stories about how they are feeling and what they are thinking. So the first thing to do is to get their faces and bodies warmed up and ready to do some work.

Core activities

Big body
Move the chairs away. Ask everyone to stand up and make their body into the biggest shape they can. Everyone in the group does this with you modelling first of all.

Now ask everyone to make their bodies into the smallest shape they can. Follow this with the saddest shape and finally, the happiest shape.

Now ask them to do the same with their faces. Start with the biggest shape, then the smallest shape followed by the saddest shape and finally the happiest shape.

Now, if it is appropriate, ask them to do the same with sounds. Start with the smallest sound, then the biggest sound, followed by the happiest sound and finally the saddest sound.

If the children are signing ask them to make the smallest sign, biggest sign, happiest sign and saddest sign.

4

Now ask the children to put some of these together. You are aiming for them to eventually be able to show:

- biggest face, biggest body and biggest sound or sign
- smallest face, smallest body and smallest sound or sign
- saddest face, saddest body and saddest sound or sign
- happiest face, happiest body and happiest sound or sign.

Encourage the children in their work and explain that now they are going on to use their bodies and faces in some drama work.

Getting into pairs

Explain to the group that in a few seconds you will give each of them a piece of paper with a word on it. This word will help them find the partner they are going to work with for the next exercise. When each person in the group has their piece of paper with a word on it they will try to find the person who has a matching or opposite word to theirs, for example, night goes with day, bread with butter and salt with pepper. On your instruction, all the children will stand up and find the person with the matching word.

Ask the group to stand with their partner in the room. (Use the CD-ROM sheet Getting into pairs.)

Pairs – still images

Explain that you are going to call out different types of people, in different situations, and each pair will have five seconds to make themselves into frozen statues of the people you tell you to be. Model with a pair of children, or with your teaching assistant first.

Here are the frozen statues for the pairs to make:

- Friends meeting in the street
- Friends sharing a secret
- Friends not speaking to/communicating with each other
- Friends saying/signing goodbye to each other
- Friends in trouble standing outside the head's office.

After they have done this, ask the children to sit down where they can see you. Now 'talk through' each of the images they made and discuss what feelings would have been present in each of those situations.

How do you feel meeting a friend? Happy, excited? How do you feel sharing a secret? You could feel really excited and even proud that someone has chosen you to trust with their secret.

How do you feel when you are arguing? Angry?

What other words might describe anger? Furious, mad?

How do you feel when you're not speaking to someone? Sulky, moody?

Extend the emotional vocabulary through this exercise. Scribe on the flipchart lots of possible words for a particular feeling.

Save this flipchart sheet for the next session.

End activity

'Something I've enjoyed today'
Explain that it is nearly the end of the drama session, but to finish off you are going to pass the talking object around the circle and each person will complete the sentence 'Something I've enjoyed today is . . . ' and pass around the talking object you used in the first name round.

Getting into pairs

bread	butter	sun	moon
night	day	hammer	nail
salt	pepper	cat	dog
knife	fork	cup	saucer
hat	coat	fish	chips

Using Drama to Teach Personal, Social and Emotional Skills, Paul Chapman Publishing, A Lucky Duck Book © Jacqui O'Hanlon and Angie Wootten, 2007.

Session 2: Exploring Feelings

Objectives

- To establish a feelings vocabulary with a corresponding range of movements.
- To begin to discuss how our feelings change.

Materials and preparation

- Flipchart sheet from last session with emotional vocabulary (for *'How am I feeling?'*).
- Use the resource *'Feelings'*. The whole group is divided into four. You will need enough pieces of paper with one word on it for each group (for use in the game *'Feeling walks'*).

Introductory name game

Name and something I like doing
(This may not be a suitable game for signing children. Please choose another from the *Name games* or *Affirmation games* section of the Compendium of Games.)

Make sure that everyone is seated in a circle. Explain to the children that they will each say or sign their name and then do an action for something they like doing. Model this by saying/signing, for example, 'I'm Miss Butler and I like singing'. Make an action for 'singing', but don't say the word. The group will then say out loud what the action is. Then the next person in the circle will say, 'I'm Mrs Best and I like (mime/sign for walking)'. This will continue around the circle, with the group naming the action each time.

Process   Ask the group whether they noticed anything in that game? It might be that they mention how people like different things or how hard they need to concentrate to remember other people's contributions.

Follow on from this to a co-operative group game.

Co-operative group game

Follow the leader (detective)
(Preface this game by playing 'Follow the leader', with yourself as the leader, and modelling different kinds of actions. Then ask the group how they could disguise who was leading the actions.)

Keep in a circle but in this game one child (the detective) leaves the room. In their absence a leader of movements is chosen. This leader starts doing actions that everyone else in the room copies, for example, tapping knees, clapping hands, stamping feet. The leader should change actions as often as possible to maintain interest. The child who has left the room is the detective and their task, on being invited back into the centre of the circle, is to identify who is leading all the actions. The group needs to make it difficult for the detective to guess, for example, by choosing to look at someone else rather than the leader.

Core activities

'How am I feeling?'
Refer the children back to the flipchart with the emotional vocabulary from the previous session. Choose a word, for example, 'sad' and say or sign. Model the corresponding facial expression. Tell the children you are going to point to other words and say or sign them and you want them to make the corresponding facial expression. Call expressions faster and faster. If a word is pointed to which is not understood by all you may need to demonstrate it and explain it.

Now it is the turn of the group. In the circle, a child chooses a word from the chart for the person on their left to respond to with the appropriate facial expression and upper body posture. That same person who has responded then chooses a word for the next person and so on around the circle getting faster and faster!

Feeling walks
Ideally, split the whole group into four groups and give each group a piece of paper with a feeling word on it using *'Feelings'* from the CD-ROM. Each group has to decide on a way of walking in the manner of that feeling. Appropriate feelings to start with might be 'Shy', 'Lonely', 'Moody', 'Worried'.

Each group shows their feeling to the rest of the class and the audience guesses which feeling they are demonstrating.

Swapping feelings

Divide all the children in the group into two groups. Ask the two groups to line up facing each other against opposite walls. Each group will have an opposite feeling word, for example, happy and sad, angry and calm, excited and bored, and shy and confident. Make it clear to the whole group what the two words are. Both groups walk across the room towards each other doing their feeling walk but when they meet each other halfway across the room, they must swap feelings so they carry on walking the remainder of their way in the manner of the other group's feeling. Try this a few times with different, opposite feelings.

Process Gather the children around you and ask the children if they can think of times when they swap feelings really quickly? When might they go from feeling really moody or cross, to happy and excited?

Co-operative group game

Spin the plate

A player comes into the middle of the circle and spins a plate on the floor. He or she calls out/signs a name of another member of the group who has to get to the plate and pick it up before it drops to the floor. If this new player succeeds, then he or she spins the plate and calls out another name . . . and so the game continues. To make it more complex, the player can call out/sign two names and both players called have to try to beat each other to get to the plate first.

End game

Mexican wave

The group is all seated in a circle. One person stands up with their hands in the air and quickly sits down. As soon as they sit down the person next to them stands up with their hands in the air . . . this is repeated all round the circle as quickly as possible.

Feelings

upset	shy
frightened	lonely
surprised	moody
excited	worried
disappointed	angry
grumpy	sulky
proud	cheerful
bored	joyful

Using Drama to Teach Personal, Social and Emotional Skills, Paul Chapman Publishing, A Lucky Duck Book © Jacqui O'Hanlon and Angie Wootten, 2007.

Session 3: Showing Feelings

Objectives

- To continue to explore different feelings in different situations.
- To identify events and situations that trigger particular emotions.

Materials and preparation

- Use *'Feelings'* from the CD-ROM. Print and cut up to give one word to each small group of between three and five children (for the exercise *'Showing how we feel'*).

Introductory name game

Name and feeling
Make sure the children are in a circle. In this game the idea is that each child will show how they are currently feeling. Model this by saying/signing for example, 'I'm Mr Cunningham and I'm feeling (mime action)'. Continue around the circle in the same way. At the end of the round, ask the group what feelings they saw. There will probably be a range of feelings including sleepy, sad, happy and angry.

Mixing-up game

'The sun shines on . . . '
For this game the circle of chairs needs to be widened to create a semicircle. Turn your chair out of the semicircle and stand in a position in front of the semicircle so that everyone can see you. The idea of this game is that everyone moves who falls into the category that you present. For example, say or sign, 'The sun shines on everyone who can ride a bike'. All the children who can ride a bike then change places with one another and you find a place as well. The new person standing has to carry on the game with their own phrase starting with 'The sun shines on . . . '.

Ask the group if they can remember what happened in the last session. Ask one of the group to call out any of the feelings they can remember from the last session and for the rest of the group to do the face and body action to match it. Tell the group that they're going to do some work in small groups now.

Core activity

Showing how we feel

Divide the group into small groups of between three to five children. Explain that each group will be given a feeling word (*'Feelings'* from the CD-ROM). This time the group are to act out a situation where someone is experiencing that feeling. For example, if a group is given the word 'lonely', they might act out a scene where lots of children are playing together in the playground but one person is standing on their own. Or for 'excited' they might act out a birthday party scene where one person is being given lots of presents. The children can use words in the scene if they wish, but should concentrate on body language and facial expressions to show how everyone is feeling. Give the groups three minutes to practise their scene.

Each group shows its work.

Process   Ask the audience, after each showing, what they liked about what they saw. What did they think that group did well? Take a couple of things from each group. Encourage the audience to think about what feelings they are seeing in each group's work.

Co-operative game

I sit in the woods

A circle of chairs is needed, with one extra chair. Everyone sits in the circle. There will be two children on either side of the empty chair. On a prearranged signal from you, both children will try to sit on the empty chair. The first person to get there sits on the chair and says/signs 'I sit . . .'. The person who now has the empty chair next to them moves into it and says 'in the woods'. A third person moves into the empty chair and tells the group 'and I choose X (name) to sit next to me'. The named person now moves into the seat next to their friend. At this the whole process begins again. The two children on either side of the empty chair try to race to sit on it first. The first one to succeed says or signs 'I sit', and so on as before. No leader is needed after the first signal from the teacher, as the game leads itself – an empty chair is an invitation to move. The children will enjoy racing to get into the chair and need to be warned to be careful that no one is hurt.

End games

Feelings and events

Stay in a circle. Choose a feeling that you can identify as one that the children experience on a regular basis. Ask them to communicate in the final round about what situations trigger that feeling in them. For example, 'I feel angry when . . . ' or 'I feel jealous when . . . '.

Tell the children that they are now finishing the programme of work about their own feelings. Tell them that it is good to be able to express how they feel. Encourage them to tell you, assistants and other members of the group how they are feeling from now on. You will be asking them how they are feeling. Explain that you want to end on a happy note by playing the next game.

Pass the smile

Explain that everyone needs to have a very serious face to start playing this game! You the leader will then look at the person next to you and smile at them, they then turn and pass the smile on to the person sitting next to them, and so on around the circle until everyone has smiled.

Feelings

upset	shy
frightened	lonely
surprised	moody
excited	worried
disappointed	angry
grumpy	sulky
proud	cheerful
bored	joyful

Using Drama to Teach Personal, Social and Emotional Skills, Paul Chapman Publishing, A Lucky Duck Book © Jacqui O'Hanlon and Angie Wootten, 2007.

Module Two
'I Know How You Feel'

This three-session module builds on the previous module 'I Can Express How I Feel'. It gives children the opportunity to think about the feelings of others. It encourages them to experience the feelings involved in certain situations and by people other than themselves. They are given the chance to discover that we often react similarly to certain situations. Finally, from the basis of that knowledge, they are encouraged to respond in an appropriate manner to that which others are experiencing, so showing empathy for that person. Within this module games are included which are designed to continue building the co-operative skills of drama without having direct connection with the subject matter.

Session 1: Recognising Feelings

Objectives

- To use the feelings vocabulary established in the first module.
- To explore the 'stories behind' feelings.
- To discuss the different reasons people might have for a feeling.

Materials and preparation

- Use *'Feelings sculptures'* from the CD-ROM to create small cut-up cards with one word on each of them. You will need enough cards for each pair to have one. (For use in the core activity *'Feelings sculptures'*.)

Introductory name game

Name and action
Ask the children to sit in a circle. In this game each person in the circle says or signs their name and completes an action with hands, arms, legs or feet. Start off the game by telling the group, for example, 'I'm Mrs Hickman' and then touching your head with both hands. The rest of the group says or signs their name and does their own action. Carry on around the circle in this way.

Process   Ask the group what they noticed during the game. Perhaps they noticed that everyone had very different actions, showing their individuality, or perhaps they chose similar actions, showing how much we are like each other.

Tell the children that in this module they are going to be finding out whether they are like each other in their **feelings** or not. First they are going to play a game to mix them up.

Mixing-up game

'How do you like your neighbour?'
Have the children sit in a semicircle and remove one chair. One child stands where he or she can be seen by all in the space. This child says or signs to someone sitting in the semicircle, for example, 'Rachel, how do you like your neighbour?' She says/signs 'Fine, but I'd like to change them for X and X'. She names two other people in the group. The two named people swap places with the two children sitting either side of Rachel, and the child standing up in the space tries to sit in one of the chairs as

Module Two

the children swap places thus leaving a different person in the space. The game starts again with the new standing person going to another child in the semicircle and saying/signing 'How do you like your neighbour?' and so on.

Core activity

Feelings sculptures
Use the small *'Feelings Sculptures'* cards for this exercise.

Gather the children in a semicircle around you with a space in front of you.

Tell the children that they are going to do some drama about why people have different feelings. Ask one of the children to volunteer to show everyone what they are going to be doing next. Tell the children that you are a sculptor and that the volunteer is a lump of clay! Tell them that you are going to make a wonderful work of art out of the lump of clay. All that the child has to do is let you put him or her into a position. Make a quick, accessible image, for example someone with one hand on their chest, one arm pointing upwards and looking upwards in the same direction. Ask the children to tell you what they think the story is behind the sculpture. Why is it in this position? What has happened to this person? Get ideas from the group.

Tell the children that now it is their turn. You are going to get them into pairs and label each member of the pair 'A' or 'B'. Do this. Tell the 'A's that they are going to be sculptors first but that they will all have a go. Tell the 'A's that they have got 30 seconds to make the 'B's into completely different statues to the one you made. Start. When the time is nearly up, give a count down of five, four, three, two, one, freeze. Ask 'A's to step away from their statues and 'B's to stay where they are. Now 'A's can walk around this new art gallery they have created and look at all the exhibits. What kinds of stories can they see as they walk around the art gallery?

After a minute or so, ask 'A's to go back to their partners and tell 'B's to relax. Now 'B's can 'get their own back', but they are going to do something slightly different. 'B's are going to be given a **feeling word** and they are going to sculpt 'A's into that feeling. It could be sad, or excited, or lonely, or frightened. Model this with an assistant. Hand out the labels with the feeling words on them. Pay attention to facial expressions to really convey how someone might look when they are experiencing that feeling.

When you think they have had enough time, give another count down, 'Five, four, three, two, one, freeze'. The 'B's can now walk around this new art gallery.

While 'B's are walking around, choose three separate statues that interest you and put them together. Tell the rest of the group to relax and come and sit on the floor in front of the three statues. Tell the group that these three statues make one new picture. Ask the group if they have got any ideas about what the story is behind the statues. What relationship do they have with each other and why are they all in the positions they are in? What has happened to make them feel the way they do? Encourage the children to think of completely new stories.

Ask the group to come back and sit in a circle.

Process Open a discussion by telling the children that there are many different reasons why people feel the way they do. For example, why might someone feel frightened? Why might someone feel surprised? Why might someone feel disappointed?

Allow a few minutes for suggestions and discussion.

End game

Group whoop
Explain that everyone will put the tips of their fingers on the floor and from that position will begin to rise up until they are standing with their hands stretched up high. As they rise up they will make a corresponding sound that grows as they grow until ending with a big whoop when they are standing with hands stretched up. It should go very quickly and only take a few seconds to do.

(This may not be an appropriate game for signing children so choose another game from the Compendium of Games.)

Feelings sculptures

angry	happy
upset	excited
moody	joyful
stroppy	thrilled
stressed	ecstatic
sad	scared
unhappy	shy
lonely	nervous
disappointed	anxious
frightened	frustrated

Using Drama to Teach Personal, Social and Emotional Skills, Paul Chapman Publishing, A Lucky Duck Book ©
Jacqui O'Hanlon and Angie Wootten, 2007.

Session 2: How Do I Know What You Feel?

Objectives

- To explore different feelings behind positive and negative situations.
- To explore how we know what people are feeling.

Materials and preparation

- Pairs of pictures (found on the CD-ROM *'Pictures'*). You should have enough for each child to have one picture. (For use in 'How are you feeling?')
- Flipchart sheet with a range of emotional literacy vocabulary on it, for example, angry, disappointed. Choose words that the children have previously encountered. (For use in 'How are you feeling?')
- Christmas or birthday cards cut into four pieces (if you have a very small group cut the cards into three pieces). Provide enough for one for each child. (For use in *'Feelings improvisation'*.)
- Use *Feelings improvisation* (CD-ROM). Cut up the resulting sheet to provide one scenario for each group Choose scenarios which you feel are particularly relevant to your group. (For the core activity *'Feelings improvisation'*.)

Introductory name game

'How are you feeling?'

Randomly give out all the pictures. Each child finds the other child with the same shape and sits next to that child. The pairs sit together around the circle. Refer to the flipchart sheet with 'emotional literacy vocabulary' on it. Label one member of the pair 'A', and the other 'B'. Model what the children are to do, with a learning assistant. Member 'A', the assistant, adopts a facial expression and upper body posture suggestive of a feeling. You, as 'B', introduce your partner, identifying their feeling, for example, 'This is Mrs X and she's feeling moody'. Ask the children to continue this pattern around the circle. (The pairs do not need to discuss beforehand what feeling they will be modelling.) Encourage the children to base their expressions on the work you completed with them in the first module or, if they need to, refer to the words on the flipchart. Now swap over. 'A' partners become 'B' and vice versa.

Tell the children that they are now going to play a mixing-up game to get them ready for the next part.

A co-operative group game

Fruitbowl
Arrange the circle into a semicircle. Give everyone the name of a fruit, for example, apple, orange, pear and banana. Sit at the head of the semicircle so that everyone can see you. Explain that you are going to call out a fruit and everyone who is that fruit must move and must swap places with another person who is that fruit. Practise this. Then turn your chair out of the semicircle. This time the person standing will call out/sign a fruit and will try and sit on a chair as the others move, so leaving a new person standing to call out/sign another fruit. If the person standing calls out 'Fruitbowl', everyone swaps seats.

Core activities

School scenarios – still images
Organise the children into small groups of between four and six children and ask them to sit around you where they can see you. Remind them that in the previous session they made sculptures in pairs to show different feelings. Tell them that in this session you would like them to work in their groups to show some things that can go on at school that give people different feelings. Explain that you are going to describe different types of people, in different situations and with different feelings. They will have ten seconds to make themselves into **frozen statues** of the people showing how they are feeling by their facial expressions and body language. Model with a group and give them five seconds to make a group of people at a fireworks display or a football match.

Tell them that, in their groups, they all now have ten seconds to make a statue of: *Children on a wet playtime.*

Then: *Children in the playground on a good day (when things are going well).*

Finally: *Children in the playground on a bad day (when things are going badly).*

Process Ask the children what they noticed about what happened in the group when it was wet playtime? What kinds of shapes did people make with their bodies? How did their faces look? (What happened to the distance between people/the direction they were looking in?)

Repeat for the other two scenarios.

Ask the group what we look for to see how people are feeling? Write up on the board: faces, expressions, bodies.

24

Feelings improvisation

To encourage the children into random groups give each child a Christmas or birthday card piece. Tell them all to go around silently and find the people who have corresponding pieces of the card and so form a group.

In their small groups, each group is given a scenario to act out from *'Feelings improvisation'* from the CD-ROM. Tell the groups they cannot use words in their piece – they simply convey through action what is happening paying particular attention to the feelings of those involved.

Ask each group to show its work. Ask the other children what they thought was happening? What feelings did they see? Discuss the feelings of the 'injured party' but also discuss the feelings of the other members of the group. For example, the person who is left out of the game may feel sad and lonely. However, the group of children who have rejected them may have different feelings about what they have done. Some of them may feel guilty about it. Also discuss with the children what they could do to make the situation better. How could they change the feelings of some of the children for the better?

Co-operative game

Follow the leader (detective)

(Preface this game by playing 'Follow the leader', with yourself as the leader, and modelling different kinds of actions. Then ask the group how they could disguise who was leading the actions.)

Keep in a circle but in this game one child (the detective) leaves the room. In their absence a leader of movements is chosen. This leader starts doing actions that everyone else in the room copies, for example, tapping knees, clapping hands, stamping feet. The leader should change actions as often as possible to maintain interest. The child who has left the room is the detective and their task, on being invited back into the centre of the circle, is to identify who is leading all the actions. The group need to make it difficult for the detective to guess, for example by choosing to look at someone else rather than the leader.

End activity

Pass the squeeze

All the children need to sit close to each other in a circle and link hands. The leader sends a squeeze to his left or right and the squeeze is passed around the circle until it returns to the leader.

Pictures

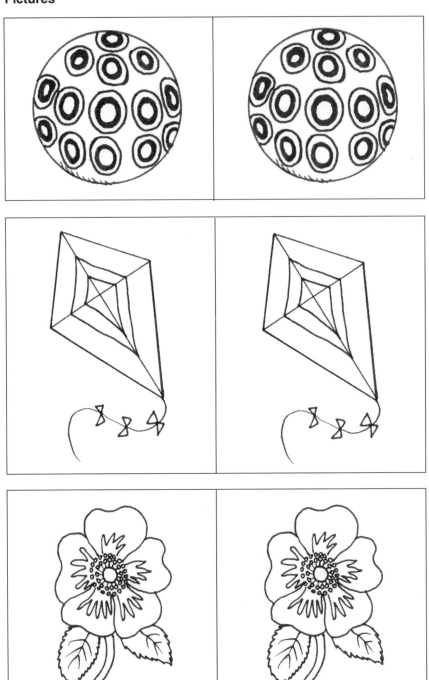

Using Drama to Teach Personal, Social and Emotional Skills, Paul Chapman Publishing, A Lucky Duck Book © Jacqui O'Hanlon and Angie Wootten, 2007.

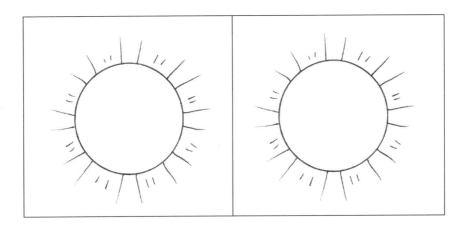

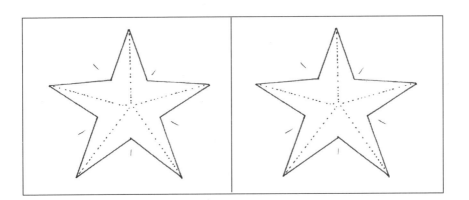

Feelings improvisation

> A group of people are playing together. Another child wants to join in but the other children tell he can't play.

> A group of children start to spread rumours about another child.

> Two friends argue with each other and then one of them goes off with other friends.

> Some children are in trouble and are standing outside the headteacher's office. They are being told off by the headteacher.

> During playtime, one child follows another child around and keeps pushing her and touching her on the shoulder.

> It is a child's first day at a new school and he does not know anybody. Children meet him in the playground before the school day has started.

> A child is walking down the corridor. Some other children bump into that child on purpose.

Using Drama to Teach Personal, Social and Emotional Skills, Paul Chapman Publishing, A Lucky Duck Book © Jacqui O'Hanlon and Angie Wootten, 2007.

Session 3: Knowing How to Respond

Objectives

- To explore the idea of responding appropriately to other people's feelings.
- To understand that we experience similar feelings.

Materials and preparation

- A tin can (for use in 'Pass the can').
- Use resource: I know how to respond: first round (from the CD-Rom). You will need one scenario per pair of children. (For use in 'I know how to respond'.)
- Use resource: I know how to respond: second round (from the CD-Rom). You will need one scenario per pair of children. (For use in 'I know how to respond'.)

Introductory name game – affirmation game

Sharks
Ask the children to form a standing circle. A player enters the circle and is the shark. She says aloud (or signs) the name of another member of the circle as she swims towards them. That person becomes the shark and their place in the circle is taken by the old shark. The new shark says/signs aloud the name of another member of the circle and swims towards them, and so on. Gradually, introduce two or even three sharks into the 'pool' at the same time.

Co-operative game

Pass the can

– quoit

Get the children to form a seated circle. Showing the group the large empty can explain that they are all going to help pass the tin can around the circle. However, no one can use their hands or arms to do this, only their feet and legs.

Place the can on your foot and send it to the person on your left or right. The aim is for it to get back to you without being dropped on the floor.

Core activity

Instant images – what would it feel like?
Move the chairs away and ask the children to move around the space. They should move briskly, making sure they keep an even spread of bodies at all times in the space. At a given signal from the leader the

players will stop walking and individually make a physical image over three seconds in response to a title by the leader. They will then freeze. Players are asked to convey through their image how they would feel in any of the given situations. Comment appropriately on a few of the images.

Suggested images:

- first day at school
- being in the naughty corner at nursery
- after an argument with your parents
- watching a scary film.

Go around and ask children questions if it is unclear what their body shapes and facial expressions are conveying. For example, 'I see you are curled up. What are you feeling?'

Process Tell the children they can relax. Bring them around you. Discuss with the children the choices they made. Many of them will be similar. Ask the children if they noticed any similarities in what they were doing – even though they could not properly see what everyone was doing. Discuss how there were a lot of similar shapes in the floor space and therefore very similar feelings. Use this idea – that we have similar reactions and feelings to each other – in the next exercise.

Core activity

'I know how to respond'
Use *'I know how to respond: first round'* from the CD-ROM. Get the children into pairs. Within the pair each child will be labelled 'A' or 'B'. In this exercise they will be given a scenario where person 'A' has a 'problem'. 'B' is going to identify how 'A' is feeling and say (or sign) something appropriate to him or her, for example 'A' has fallen over in the playground. 'B' walks over to him and says/signs, 'You look upset. Do you want me to get the teacher?' Model an example with an assistant. You may wish to write up the construction, 'You look . . . (and a corresponding remark)'. Tell the children you would like them to use this construction. Give each pair a scenario. Give them one minute to practise their scenarios.

Process Let each pair show its work to the rest of the group. Tell the rest of the children what has happened to 'A' before the pair shows their piece. Ask the children whether 'B' was right about the feeling he or she identified. Do they think that 'B' said/signed something that went well with 'A's feeling? What else could 'B' have said/signed? Once everyone has had a go at this, swap over the roles and give out some new scenarios ('*I know how to respond: second round*') where 'B' is the person with the 'problem' and 'A' must guess their feeling and respond appropriately.

Process   Go through the same process as before with the first scenarios.

Tell the children that this is the end of the drama on this subject. Tell them that you hope to see them trying to understand their friends' feelings and saying or signing the right thing. Tell them that you will be very happy if any one of them is able to tell you or the teacher what one of their friends is feeling. (There will be plenty of other opportunities to practise this skill in following modules, particularly in Module Three, 'I Can Make Friends'.)

End game

Circle mayhem
This is a game about making eye contact with someone else across the circle. In this game, eye contact is very important because once you've made eye contact with a person you swap places with them. You, as leader, take your chair out of the circle, once you have explained the game, so there will always be one person without a seat. That person can try to sit down when other people get up to swap places. Remind the group they can only swap places with one person when they have made eye contact with them.

End activity

'Something I like about being in this group is . . . '
While still in a circle, invite each child to express something that they have enjoyed about being in the group and doing this drama.

I know how to respond:

first round

> A has been left out of a game.
> How is A feeling? How will you respond, B?

> Children have been saying nasty things about A.
> How is A feeling? How will you respond, B?

> A has had a row with her best friend. The best friend has gone off with someone else.
> How is A feeling? How will you respond, B?

> Somebody has bumped into A in the corridor on purpose. B saw it happen.
> How is A feeling? How will you respond, B?

> A is being picked on by someone in the playground. A child keeps following them around and tapping them and pushing. B saw it.
> How is A feeling? How will you respond, B?

second round

> It's B's birthday and he is wearing a badge saying 'I am 9.'
> How is B feeling? How will you respond, A?

> B has come top in spelling for the first time.
> How is B feeling? How will you respond, A?

> B has got a new pet dog.
> How is B feeling? How will you respond, A?

> It is B's first day at a new school.
> How is B feeling? How will you respond, A?

> B has got a spelling test to do and she does not feel very confident about it.
> How is B feeling? How will you respond, A?

Using Drama to Teach Personal, Social and Emotional Skills, Paul Chapman Publishing, A Lucky Duck Book © Jacqui O'Hanlon and Angie Wootten, 2007.

Module Three
'I Can Make Friends'

The aim of this five-session module is to introduce the children to some of the skills of friendship. It also allows them to practise them through games and exercises. The module starts with sessions on showing interest in what our friends tell us about themselves, then moves on to sharing and, finally, trust. In the final sessions it builds on the module 'I Know How You Feel' with its emphasis on 'empathy' as an element of friendship.

Session 1: Showing Interest

Objectives

- To encourage an appreciation that they have things 'in common'.
- To encourage an understanding of the role that 'showing interest' has in making and retaining friends.

Materials and preparation

- Flipchart and pens.
- Use *'Who is the same?'* from the CD-ROM. You will need one copy for each child. (For use with the activity. *'Who is the Same?'*)
- Use the resource *'Remembering is important'* (CD-ROM). You will need one copy from which each triad will have one scenario. (For use with the activity *'Remembering is important'*.)
- Large, baked bean or coffee tin.

Introductory name game

Hobbies

The aim of this game is to encourage children to think about their hobbies, or things that they like doing, and to remember one hobby of someone else.

First get the children to think about their own hobby and what mime they will use to represent it. (Deaf signing children will use signs.)

Have the children sit in a circle, ideally with an assistant to your left. Start off, for example saying, 'I'm Miss Smith and I like . . . (do the mime or sign for swimming)'. The assistant to the left then says or signs, 'This is Miss Smith and she likes . . . (mime or sign). I'm Mrs Jackson and I like . . . (mime or sign)'. The next child to the left around the circle has to remember Mrs Jackson's hobby before she or he says or signs his own. Go all around the circle.

Mixing-up game

All change

The aim of this game is to encourage the children to see the areas of life that they have in common with each other. Encourage the children to move out into a semicircle then sit at the head of the shape where everyone can see you. Call out or sign, for example, 'All change anyone who likes football'. At this all the children who like football must change places. Choose elements that are either hobbies or favourites, likes or dislikes for future elements of this lesson. During one of the changes sit down yourself, therefore leaving a child as 'caller'. Encourage the child to choose similar types of commonalities.

Make sure you are at last the 'caller' and shout 'All change' allowing all the children to get up and change seats.

Sit where everyone can see you. Tell the children, in your own words, that they are going to be exploring friendship and its skills in your drama sessions in the next few sessions. At this point you may like to ask the children what makes a good friend and record their ideas on a flipchart. Children tend to find this a difficult question so it may be helpful to give them some ideas, for example, 'Is it good to hit or tell lies about your friend?' 'What does a good friend do?' Record their ideas on a flipchart sheet, particularly highlighting skills to be covered in the next sessions.

Tell the children that today they are going to be thinking about attending to what our friends tell us about themselves and remembering that information. Also tell them that this is an important aspect of friendship.

Core activities

'Who is the same?'

Tell the children that first of all they are going to play a game where they find out about people in the group by asking questions. Explain that they may find that they have things in common with each other.

Present the children with the sheet *'Who is the same?'* Tell the children that they are going to go round trying to find out who has the same favourite foods, colours, TV programmes as them by asking each child in the group. It will be advisable for the children first to write down their **own** favourite colour, hobby, food in the **second** of the pair of blank lines before going round the group. Ask the children what questions they will ask and, if necessary, model with an assistant or child. When a child receives an answer, he should compare it with his own answer for that question. If it is the same then the name of the child who has answered should be written in the **first** of the pair of blank lines.

The children should go round all members of the group for each question. This way they will have plenty of practice in asking questions.

Process Ask the children whether they have learned anything about anyone they didn't know before. What have they found out? Ask for examples. Now ask the children to turn their papers face down and tell you anything they can remember about someone else. When child A tells you something about child B, ask child B how it feels that child A has remembered something about him or her. Encourage them to see that it makes them feel special and that someone is interested in them. Tell the children to have a look at their sheets again and try to remember something about someone else for the next session.

Tell the children that sometimes it is very important that we remember things about our friends. They are now going to play another game to show this.

Remembering is important
Get the children, or children and assistants, into triads. Each triad is given a scenario from *'Remembering is important'*. Each triad is asked to create a scene using the situation described to show to the other groups. The triads should rehearse together for two minutes and then show to the other groups. During the scene, make clear to the children that each person can only express themselves once and there should be a clear start and end image.

Process Ask the children what would have happened if the child **had** remembered the information. Conclude that it's important to remember what our friends tell us.

End activity

Pass the can
Get the children to form a circle. Use a large, empty baked beans can, or similar. (These can often be found in school kitchens.) Explain that you are all going to help pass the tin can around the circle. However, no one can use their hands or arms to do this, only their feet and legs. Place the can on your foot and send it to the person on your left or right. The aim is for it to get back to you without being dropped on the floor.

Who is the same?

	Other person	My answer
Who has the same favourite colour as you?	....	....
Who has the same hobby as you?	....	....
Who has the same favourite food as you?	....	....
Who was born in the same month as you?	....	....
Who has the same favourite TV programme as you?	....	....
Who has the same favourite lesson as you?	....	....
Who has the same favourite cartoon as you?	....	....
Who has the same favourite ice-cream as you?	....	....
Who has the same favourite song as you?	....	....
Who has the same favourite animal as you?	....	....

Using Drama to Teach Personal, Social and Emotional Skills, Paul Chapman Publishing, A Lucky Duck Book © Jacqui O'Hanlon and Angie Wootten, 2007.

Remembering is important

Becky's birthday is coming up. Ellie asks her the date of her birthday so that she can give her a card. Becky says it is 27 May. Ellie forgets and thinks it is 29 May. What happens on Becky's birthday?

Sam is coming to tea. Mum tells Ryan to ask Sam if there is anything he doesn't like to eat. Ryan forgets to ask Sam but pretends to his mum that he eats everything. When Sam comes, mum cooks him something that would make him very ill. Show what happens next.

Bella tells Laura that she doesn't like dogs. She is frightened of them because a dog bit her. Laura forgets. One day Laura's family gets a dog as a pet. Laura invites Bella around to play. What happens next?

Ollie is going on holiday. He asks Soham to look after his special book that he has brought into school to show the children and which they are still enjoying. Soham forgets. The children are rough with the book and tear it. What happens when Ollie gets back to school?

Zac has to stay in at playtime to finish some work. He asks Matthew if he will get a snack for him from the tuckshop and gives him the money. Matthew forgets and just buys his own. What happens when Zac meets Matthew?

Using Drama to Teach Personal, Social and Emotional Skills, Paul Chapman Publishing, A Lucky Duck Book © Jacqui O'Hanlon and Angie Wootten, 2007.

Session 2: Sharing

Objectives

- To consolidate the previous session's work on showing an interest in others.
- To explore how sharing is important for friendship.
- To give children the opportunity to share in the session.
- To explore selflessness as opposed to selfishness.

Materials and preparation

- Flipchart and pens. (For use in *'I sit in the woods'* and *'Fives'* and *'Times when we don't want to share'*.)
- Small cakes in pairs. (One cake per child.) These paired cakes are quite easy to acquire. One leading small cake manufacturer does a range. If it's not possible to get hold of these, use wrapped biscuits. (For use in *'Cakes'*.)
- If appropriate (depending on the level of hearing of the children) a CD or tape of 'upbeat' music and a CD or tape player. (For use in *'Cakes'*.)

Introductory name game

Remembering something about someone
The aim of the first game is to consolidate what was learnt in the previous session – that it's good to remember what our friends tell us because it shows that we are interested in them.

Sit in a circle. Tell the children that you are going to go round the circle and that everyone is going to try to remember one thing about someone else which they learnt in the previous session. Start off: 'I'm Mrs Wright and I remember that Rachel had the same favourite colour as me which is green.' Continue around the circle. Note the smiles of children who have had something remembered about them and mention this to the children. Praise children who have remembered something about someone else.

Mixing-up game

'I sit in the woods'
This game has been described before in Module One. Here the game is used to begin to explore how it feels to be left out.

A circle of chairs is needed with one extra chair. Everyone sits in the circle. There will be two children on either side of the empty chair. On a prearranged signal from you both children will try to sit on the empty chair. The first person to get there sits on the chair and says or signs 'I sit . . . '. The person who now has the empty chair next to them moves into it and says or signs 'in the woods'. A third person moves into the empty chair and says or signs 'and I choose X (name) to sit next to me'. The named person now moves into the seat next to their friend. At this the whole process begins again. The two children on either side of the empty chair try to sit on it first. The first one to succeed says or signs 'I sit' and so on as before. No leader is needed after the first signal from the teacher as the game leads itself – an empty chair is an invitation to move. The children will enjoy racing to get into the chair and need to be warned to be careful that no one is hurt.

Process   Ask the children the question: 'How did it feel when you didn't get to the chair?' Accept a wide range of negative emotions. Extend vocabulary as you go. You may like to consider recording these emotions on a flipchart. If so keep this sheet for Session 4.

Co-operative group game

Fives
This game explores how it feels to be 'left out'.

This time the players stand in a circle. Start by explaining that they will count from one to five around the circle and the person who says or signs 'five' has to sit down and is out of the game. Players can say or sign one or two numbers at a time. The game continues until there is only one person left standing. This person is declared the winner.

Note: If you have a very small group, including assistants, it may be necessary to increase the number from five to six, for example. This way the game lasts longer!

Process   Tell the children to sit down so that everyone can see you. Ask the children how they felt playing the game. Ask 'What was it like when the player before you said four and you knew you were going to be out?' Note down any negative emotions on the flipchart. Keep this sheet for the next activity and Session 4.

Tell the children that in that last game they sometimes had to do things that they didn't want to do. Sometimes we have to do things that we don't want to do when we share things. Tell the children that this session is about sharing.

Core activity

Times when we don't want to share
With the children, discuss and list on the flipchart five different things that we don't always want to share with our friends, for example, gel pen or football or winning games or even time with the television! Ask the children to go into pairs or groups of three and prepare a scene where one or two children do not want to share something with another child. Each pair could use one of the items you have just noted down as a basis for their scene. However, tell the children that during the scene, they may only use three words to express what it going on. They will have to convey the story of the scene through body language and intonation – either signed or vocalised – of those three words. The children will need to decide on which words to use and their ordering, as well as who says or signs which word. You may need to model this with an assistant. For example, the scenario might be two siblings fighting over the remote control as they watch television, both wanting to see different programmes.

One sibling presses the button for the channel she wants to watch.

Older sister: Yes!

The other sibling changes it back to another channel.

Younger sister: No!

The other sibling changes it to her preferred channel.

Older sister: Yes!

In addition, encourage all of the children to make a strong facial expression that shows how they are feeling at the end of the scene. In effect, each small scene will end with a frozen picture.

Ask each group to show their scene for the others to see. At the end point of the scene, encourage the watching children to explore through discussion how each person in the picture is feeling. Try to encourage children to use words from the flipchart sheet from 'Fives'.

Process   Discuss with the children how these scenes can be 'turned around' – instead of getting a negative response the child now gets a positive response. Don't be too simplistic. Allow discussion around the idea that sometimes children have to wait for something and sometimes it isn't possible for them to have what they want – for example, because it is the end of playtime.

End activities

Cakes
Bring the children back into a circle.

Give a pair of cakes or two wrapped biscuits to every other child in the group. Tell all the children that each child with the cakes or biscuits is going to share what they have with another child, who at the moment, hasn't got any. Tell the children that they could easily choose a friend but that might leave someone else out. Ask them how that would that make that person feel? Ask them to think carefully who they will choose in order to give someone a good feeling and make them smile.

Ask each child with a cake/biscuit to choose a person by saying or signing, 'I choose Ahmed'. Then the person with the cake or biscuit should go over and give that chosen person their cake or biscuit. If appropriate, put on some upbeat music and have that playing in the background as the children eat together.

Sharing challenge!
Ask all the children to find an opportunity in the time between the sessions to share something with another person. Discuss what kinds of things they might share and with whom. It might be at school or at home. Ask the children to remember what it is they have shared for a game in the next session.

Session 3: Trust

Objectives

- To consolidate the previous two sessions' work on showing interest and sharing.
- To establish that trust is important in friendships.
- To explore how important it is to feel we can rely on our friends and know that they won't let us down.

Materials and preparation

- Flipchart or whiteboard and pens (for *'Secrets scenarios'*).
- Use *'Secrets scenarios'* from the CD-ROM. Make one copy (for the activity *'Secrets scenarios'*).
- A set of small cards for the game *'Wink murder'*. Cut enough for one for each child, plus one more, (and cards for the staff). They should all be blank except two: one should have the word 'Murderer' on it and the other the word 'Detective'.

Introductory name game – affirmation game

Sharing

This game draws on the challenge given to the children at the end of the previous session – to share something with another person. It also gives the children further practice in remembering what someone else has told them.

Have the children sit in a circle, ideally with an assistant to your left. Ask the children to try to remember something that they have shared with another person in the time since the last session. Tell them that they are going to find out what other children have been sharing by asking around the circle. Start off the process by saying or signing, for example: 'My name is Mr Lilley and yesterday I shared my crisps at playtime with another teacher'. The assistant in the circle says or signs, 'This is Mr Lilley. He shared his crisps with another teacher. I'm Mrs Peterson and I lent my pen to my daughter Daisy'. Go around the circle and praise the children for sharing.

Co-operative group game

Co-operative fives

This game further challenges the children to share and consolidates the previous session.

Move the chairs away and have the children stand in a circle. Introduce a new version of the game *'Fives'*. Remind the group that in the original game they counted from one to five around the circle and the person who said 'five' had to sit down and was out of the game. Players could say or sign one or two numbers at a time. This time, with the group, elect two children that the group are now going to 'save'. These two children will be the final ones left standing at the end of the game. In order to do this, other children will have to 'sacrifice themselves' and say or sign 'five' on purpose to get themselves out in order to save the appropriate two. Remember that the children can say or sign one or two numbers.

Note: Adjust these numbers to suit the size of the group. The smaller the group the higher the number should be adjusted up from five. Also if it is a small group you may only wish to save one person.

Process Ask the children, 'How does it feel to play it like that? Is it difficult to play it like this? Why?' Hopefully you will elicit the idea that it is hard to save someone else when you know that you will lose out. Tell the children that there will be more games to practise sharing skills in later sessions. Now they are going to move on to a new skill of friendship.

Core activities

Chinese movement game

The next part of the session is about trust.

The aim of this game is to show how 'information' can be distorted and changed as it passes from one person to another. This leads into a discussion about trust.

This time the children should form a line one behind the other and all facing towards you at first. Tell the children that you are going to start off a movement and the next person along has to copy it, and so on down the line. It could be a series of movements, for example (1) patting your head with both hands, (2) folding your arms and (3) stamping once with each foot. Choose a sequence that suits the children's age and ability. Tell the children that they are going to turn around so that they are facing away from you and that each child will receive a tap on the shoulder as a cue to turn around to see the sequence of movements by the next child up the line. It may well be a good idea to model this with an assistant.

All the children should turn away except for the child at the head of the line in front of you. Do your sequence of movements in front of this child. Each child has to copy, as well as they can, the movement sequence. The idea is to see what the movement sequence has become at the end and to see how close this new version is to the original. It is often very different.

Ask your assistant to go to the other end of the line to ensure that there is no peeping on the part of the children waiting!

If there is time, let a child start a sequence and 'pass it down the line' in the same way.

Process Get the children to come and sit where they can see you on chairs and discuss what they saw. The more you pass something on the more it changes. Discuss with the children how this is a bit like what happens when we tell tales about our friends. You might have to illustrate with pictures here or model with two assistants. For example, start off a story which changes from 'Jessica's got two Easter eggs and she's eating both', to 'Jessica's got two Easter eggs and she won't share them'. Ask the children how Jessica would feel if she found out what was being said. These people are supposed to be her friends but they are telling tales about her. She won't be able to **trust** them. Tell the children that this session is about trust.

The same thing can happen with secrets. Explain to the children that you are going to give them a title of a picture. The title is: 'Sharing a secret'. Invite children to enter the empty space and strike an image of something connected with this title. One child will enter and strike a pose – perhaps crouching down with their finger to their lips – then another child will add onto this image. Once an image is clearly established that looks like the picture title, tell the group the picture is now complete. Ask the 'audience' to process the identities and feelings of everyone in the picture, for example, who is telling the secret? How does that person feel? How do the people feel who are being told the secret? Who are the people who are being told? There may be quite a lot of complex, different feelings involved.

Secrets scenarios
Discuss with the children how sometimes friends tell each other secrets. Discuss what sort of secrets these might be and write them up on a whiteboard or flipchart sheet. There are some ideas in *'Secrets scenarios'*

from the CD-ROM. You may like to choose a few to stimulate the children's thoughts

Tell the children they are going to get into groups of three. One friend is going to tell a secret to another. It is up to each group to decide which of the 'secrets' they choose from the list. The friend then goes to a third person and tells them the secret, perhaps adding some extra things to make it more important – or saying or signing something nasty about them. Ask the group to decide on what is said. Model with a teaching assistant and child, or ask three volunteers to try one out. Give the children a limited time to practise their scene (two to three minutes) and then each group shows the other groups their work.

Process   Discuss with the children how this makes the first person (who has told the secret) feel. Is the second person being a good friend? If not, why not? Bring in the word 'trust' again. Discuss with the children what you should do if your friend tells you a secret.

Use the flipchart or whiteboard and pens. Ask the children to tell you situations where we lose our trust in friends, for example, when someone breaks a toy that another child has lent them. Ask the children what they, as friends, should do instead in each instance, for example, be careful to look after someone else's things.

End activity

Wink murder
Sit in a circle. Practise winking first! Hold the cards face down (keep the detective card out at first) and invite each child to take a card at random and not to reveal what is on their card. Tell the children that someone is the murderer and is going to try to 'kill' everyone in the group by winking at them. The children must look around at everyone and if they are 'winked at' they have to fold their arms and bow their heads because they are 'dead'.

Have one complete game and let the murderer 'kill' everyone if he or she can. Then play the game again, this time introducing the detective card. The child who gets this card is required to work out who the murderer is as soon as possible and stop that person 'killing' any more people.

Secrets scenarios

My mum's having a baby but don't tell anyone.

I'm frightened of spiders but don't tell anyone.

I'm going for a sleepover at Gavin's but don't tell anyone.

The police came to our house last night but don't tell anyone.

I put my hearing aid in my pocket and my mum put my trousers in the washing machine. Now it doesn't work but don't tell anyone.

I can't swim but don't tell anyone.

I'm coming as Harry Potter on Book Day but don't tell anyone.

I'm giving Shazia a bracelet for her birthday but don't tell anyone.

My brother's in prison but don't tell anyone.

I forgot to bring my homework but don't tell anyone.

I'm pretending my radio aid is at home but really it's in my bag – but don't tell anyone.

Using Drama to Teach Personal, Social and Emotional Skills, Paul Chapman Publishing, A Lucky Duck Book © Jacqui O'Hanlon and Angie Wootten, 2007.

Wink murder

Detective	**Murderer**

Session 4: Empathy

Objectives

- To begin to consolidate what has been learnt about the skills of friendship from previous sessions.
- To see that understanding people's feelings is an important part of friendship.
- To begin to respond to other people's feelings.

Materials and preparation

- Flipchart sheet/s from Module Two: Session 2 (*'Feelings'*)
- *'Feelings'* from the CD-ROM cut up into small cards (for *'Pairs, feelings and responses'*).
- Two large baked beans cans, or similar.

Introductory name game

'I'm a good friend'
This game starts to consolidate what has been learnt by the children about the skills of friendship in the previous sessions.

Have the children sit in a circle. Ask the group to think about all the work they have done so far on friendship. Encourage them to remember the skill practised in each session. Now ask each person to think of one thing that makes them a good friend. Tell them that you are going to go round the circle and the children are to say or sign one thing that makes them a good friend. Start with, for example: 'My name is Miss Hickey and I'm a good friend because I remember things people tell me'. And so on around the circle. If a child cannot express anything about themselves encourage the child by pointing out a skill that you've noticed they possess, for example, 'You waited for Arran while he did up his coat in the cloakroom'.

Remind the children that in the last session they had been thinking about trust. Remind them of discussing all the different feelings experienced when we were trusted or when our trust was broken. Tell the children that in this session they are going to carry on thinking about feelings, but this time about how important it is to understand and recognise how our friends are feeling.

Collaborative game

Feelings and facial expressions

Keep the children sitting in a circle. Ask each child to think of a feeling. Encourage them to be very specific about the feeling and use the flipchart sheet/s from Session 2 to extend the range of possible feelings chosen. Child X will start by modelling their feeling using facial expression and upper body language to the child on their left. This child names the feeling they are seeing and then models a new one to the person on their left, and so on around the circle.

Process Ask children if they found their neighbours were successful in naming the exact feeling they had in their minds. Explain that often we can guess correctly how people feel, but also that we can get it wrong sometimes.

Core activities

Pairs

(This activity also appeared in Module One, 'I Can Express What I Feel'. Here it is used within the context of friendship.) Tell the group that you're going to divide them into pairs and tell them a picture to act out. Every pair will form a frozen image of each picture. Tell the children you are going to give them a count-down as they form their image, for example, five, four, three, two, one, freeze.

The children divide into pairs. You call out these scenarios:

- friends who are meeting after a long time
- friends who have had an argument
- two friends; one friend won't give a toy back
- a friend whose pet rabbit has died. What does the other friend do?

Process Tell the children to sit down where they are facing you. Discuss with the children that in the last picture one person was upset or in distress. What was the other friend doing and saying (signing)? Discuss with the children that part of being a friend is knowing how to be with that person and understand their feelings.

Pairs, feelings and responses

Ask the children to find new partners. Give each pair a feeling word from *'Feelings'* (CD-ROM). Ask them to create a still image showing a situation where one of them is experiencing that emotion and the other is responding appropriately.

For example: a pair is given the feeling word 'upset'. They create an image where one of them has fallen over in the playground and the other is comforting them. Model this with an assistant.

Give the pairs two or three minutes to practise their image. Then each pair shows their still image to the rest of the group. Ask the group to guess the emotion and to also identify what the 'friend' is doing in their response. Finally, ask the pairs to bring their image to life, with each person saying or signing a line that fits their scenario.

From the original example 'upset' , their lines might be:

A: My knee really hurts. I just want to go home.
B: I'll take you to the teacher. You'll be alright in a minute.

Praise the children for their work and explain that they will be doing some more work on this next session.

End activity

Pass the cans!
Have the children sit in a circle. Tell the children that they have to pass the two tin cans around the circle using only their feet. Set one can off in one direction and the other in the other direction. There will be an interesting moment when the two cans meet!

Feelings

upset
frightened
surprised
excited
disappointed
grumpy
proud
bored

Session 5: Empathy and Affirmation

This is a short session designed to consolidate the module.

Objectives

- To consolidate the learning about empathy from Session 4.
- To highlight the importance of affirmation as promoting positive feelings in friendships.
- To consolidate the children's learning from the whole module.

Materials and preparation

- Use *'Friendship bag'* (CD-ROM). Produce one copy for each child. Or you may prefer to draw your own version on a flipchart sheet if you would like the children to work collaboratively. (For use in the activity *'Friendship bag'.*)

Introductory name game – affirmation game

Affirming someone's friendship skills

Sit in a circle. Ask everyone to think about the child sitting on their left. They should think of some quality in this person that makes them a good friend. Each child should then start and complete the following statement around the circle. For example, say or sign, 'My name is Miss Johnson and this is Dimos. He is a good friend because he helped Marsha on the playground'. After this initial example, withdraw yourself from the circle so that the children are just concentrating on each other. Prompt them as necessary and ask for suggestions from other children if a child 'gets stuck'. Try to ensure that each child has had something positive attributed to them.

Process   Come back into the circle. Ask the children how it felt to have positive things said about them. Refer to specific examples.

Tell the children that they should enjoy being paid compliments (use vocabulary here to suit the children's language level). It helps us to feel good about ourselves and about the person who expressed it! Tell the children that taking care of other people's feelings is what the session is about today.

Mixing-up game

'How do you like your neighbour?'

This game has already been described in 'I Can Express How I Feel'. However this time the aim of the game is to encourage the children to think how about which child they will choose in order to look after another child's feelings.

Have the children sit in a semicircle. One child stands where he or she can be seen by all in the space. This child says/signs to someone sitting in the semicircle, 'Rachel, how do you like your neighbour?' She says/signs, 'Fine, but I'd like to change them for X and X'. She names two other people in the group. The two named people swap places with the two children sitting either side of Rachel, and the child standing up in the space tries to sit in one of the chairs as the children swap places thus leaving a different person in the space. The game starts again with the new standing person going to another child in the semicircle and saying/signing 'How do you like your neighbour?' and so on.

Encourage the children to think about the work from the previous session about the feelings of others and to choose children they wouldn't usually choose.

Core activity

The friendship bag

Tell the children that they have now come to the end of their sessions on friendship and this is a chance for them to show what they've learnt.

Use the *'Friendship bag'* (CD-ROM). Ask the children to name as many elements as possible that go into the *'Friendship bag'* to make someone a good friend. Encourage them to refer to skills explored in each session as well as thinking for themselves. [This game is based on an original idea by WMQPEP.]

End game

Group whoop

Explain that everyone will put the tips of their fingers on the floor and from that position will begin to rise up until they are standing with their hands stretched up high. As they rise up they will make a corresponding sound that grows as they grow until ending with a big whoop when they are standing with hands stretched up. It should go very quickly and only take a few seconds to do.

(This may not be an appropriate game for signing children so choose another game from the Compendium of Games.)

Friendship bag

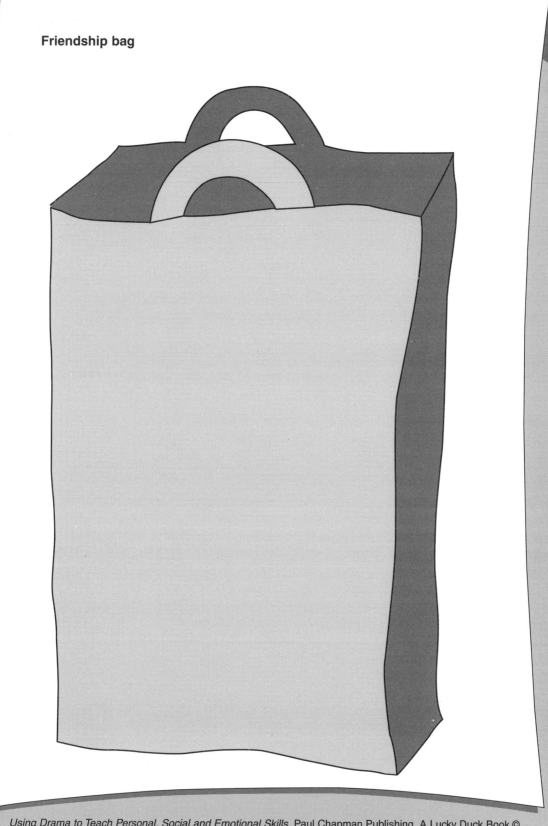

Module Four
'I Can Keep Friends'

The aim of this four-session module is to introduce ways in which friends can be kept, rather than lost. It is recognised that having friendships is a very important part of school life. Children, especially children who are deaf, lose friends for a variety of reasons including miscommunication, misunderstandings and perceiving actions to be deliberate rather than mistakes. The sessions begin with an exploration of possible causes for friendship breakdown. They go on to deal with how conflicts escalate, how feelings can be managed and how alternative reactions can be developed.

Session 1: Causes of Friendship Breakdown

Objectives

- To explore causes of friendship breakdown.
- To consider in particular the effect of insults.
- To consolidate the effect of compliments from the previous strand.

Materials and preparation

- Flipchart paper and pens (for the activities *'Causes of friendship breakdown'* and *'Compliments and insults'*).
- Plastic or tin plate.

Introductory name game – affirmation game

My best friend

Seat the children in a circle. Start by modelling a statement about your best friend, for example: 'I'm Mr Wright and my best friend is Paul'. The child to your left then says/signs, 'This is Mr Wright and his best friend is Paul. I'm Mandy and my best friend is Holly'. Continue around the circle, with each new child having to remember and make a statement about the friend of the person before them, before making a statement about themselves.

Core activities

Still images

(This activity has been used in two other modules. In this version it is used as a way to introduce conflict in a relationship.)

Get the children into pairs. Tell the children that you are going to call out different pairs of people in different situations, and they will have five seconds to make themselves into frozen statues of these pairs. Demonstrate with a pair, giving them five seconds to make a statue-pair of two friends laughing together.

Once they have got the idea, here are the statues for the children to try. Give them a five second countdown to make the statues.

- friends playing together
- friends arguing with each other
- friends not speaking to/communicating with each other.

Process Ask the children what feelings the two friends who were not communicating would have.

Explain to the children that in these sessions they will be exploring friendship, what makes friendships go wrong and how to stop that situation from happening. Ask the children which of them has fallen out with someone in the last week, month, year (being aware that it might have happened within the group!).

Causes of friendship breakdown
Tell the children that you would like them to think of five things that make them fall out or create arguments. If the children are young, you may wish to scribe for them on the flipchart. If the children are older, you may like to divide them into groups and give each group a piece of paper and a pen, appoint a scribe and give them two or three minutes to come back with their ideas. If the latter course is chosen, discuss the ideas of each group. You might increase the number of causes by additionally asking the children about things they don't like happening with their friends. Save this flipchart sheet or individual sheets for Session 2.

Compliments and insults
Use the flipchart and head two columns 'Positive' and 'Negative'.

If it hasn't already come up, discuss with the children that one of the things that can cause friendships to break is 'name-calling'. Encourage some examples from the children. Give some more examples. At the same time ask them to think about the sorts of noises we make or signs we give which show we don't like people. Scribe all these under the negative heading.

Remind the children of the work in the last module about giving compliments and ask the children to think of some positive things we could say or sign to each other. At the same time ask them to about the sorts of noises we make or signs we give which show we like people. Scribe all these under the positive heading.

You may end up with something like the example below:

Positive	Negative
Laughter	Sighs
Giggling	Yawns
Whoops	Tuts

62

Cheers	Boos
'Great'	'Rubbish'
'You're fantastic'	'Waste of time'
'Brill'	'No'
'Yeah'	'Stupid'
'Wow'	

Divide the children into two groups. Explain that each group will create a different 'sound-scape' or 'sign-scape' (depending on whether the children communicate more readily through speech or sign) to describe two different emotional states or feelings. One group will create a positive atmosphere using sounds, signs or both, and the other group will create a negative atmosphere.

Each group should be encouraged to 'layer' their sound or sign-scape so that there is a sense of it growing. One way of doing this might be to begin with one sound, sign or word by one child and gradually other sounds, words or signs said by other children will be added in so that it grows in volume and/or visual intensity. You could be the 'conductor' of the sounds or signs, pointing to each person as their sounds are needed. In essence try to achieve a beginning, middle and end for each sound- or sign-scape.

The idea is that each group should surround the other with their sound or sign-scape. Let the 'Negatives' go first. Have the 'Positives' sit on the floor of the room while they are surrounded by the 'Negatives' sounds, words or signs. Then change over. If the children are purely oral and have sufficient hearing you may like to consider encouraging the children to close their eyes and just listen to the sounds washing around them.

Process Ask the 'Positives' how they felt when the 'Negatives' were surrounding them with their sounds, words or signs. Note the emotions on a new flipchart sheet. By this time the group should be able to come up with a wide range of words to describe how they felt. Now ask the 'Negatives' to describe how they felt when the 'Positives' were surrounding them with their words or signs. Save all these words on the flipchart sheet for the next session.

End activity

Spin the plate
A player comes into the middle of the circle and spins a plate on the floor. He or she calls out or signs a name of another member of the group who

has to get to the plate and pick it up before it drops to the floor. If this new player succeeds then he or she spins the plate and calls out another name . . . and so the game continues. To make it more complex, the player can call out two names and both players called have to try to beat each other to get to the plate first.

Session 2: Conflict Escalation

Objectives

- To consolidate the work on feelings engendered by bad experiences in friendship.
- To consolidate the idea of saying/signing positive things to each other.
- To explore the way in which conflict escalates.
- To explore the growth of anger.
- To explore the difference between mistakes and planned behaviour.

Materials and preparation

- A4 paper cut into two vertical strips. Fold each strip into six, like a concertina. This is going to be a 'consequence concertina'. Prepare enough for one per pair, plus one more for demonstration purposes. Write a scenario which might set off a friendship breakdown on the top section of the demonstration strip. Examples can be found under the heading *'Consequence concertina scenarios'* at the end of this session or use the ideas from the children's *'Causes of friendship breakdown activity'* flipchart sheet from the last session. Write or stick one scenario at the top of each concertina strip. (For use in *'Consequence concertinas'.*)
- Flipchart paper with a flight of three ascending steps drawn on it. At the top write 'broken friendship'. (For use in *'Consequence concertinas'.*)
- Flipchart pens including a red one. (For use in *'Consequence concertinas'.*)
- Use *'Scenarios'* from the CD-ROM or write some of your own which you know to be appropriate to the children you are with. Each pair should have a full set. (For use in *'Mistake or not?'*)
- Spare flipchart paper (For use in *'Mistake or not?'*)
- Blu tac (For use in *'Mistake or not?'*).

Introductory name game

Compliments

Get the children to sit in a circle. Remind the children of the core activity *'Compliments and insults'* that they did in the last session. Remind them how they found out how much better compliments feel than insults. Tell them that they are going to play a game now where they think of one compliment about the person sitting on their left. Give some examples. Then start with yourself, for example, 'I'm Mrs Bates and I'm good at making marmalade. This is Ahmed and he's good at swimming'. Ahmed will say or sign, 'I'm Ahmed. I'm good at swimming. This is Sarah and she's good at taking the register to the office'. Go all round the circle, with each child repeating the information about themselves and adding a compliment about the person to their left.

Core activities

Consequence concertinas
Tell the children that they are going to explore the way in which one thing leads to another and ends with a broken friendship.

(Refer them back to the flipchart sheet from last session that showed causes of friendship break-up if you have used ideas from this for the consequence concertinas).

Show them an example of a 'consequence concertina' with a scenario at the top. It might look like this:

Consequence concertina

Example

B tripped up A in the corridor

A

B

A

B

A

Involve all the children in discussing what each person would say or sign. Record each utterance of the dialogue on a new step until you have a whole sequence. It might look like this:

Consequence concertina

Example

B tripped up A in the corridor

A: Watch it!

B: You should look where you're going.

A: You stuck your foot out.

B: Didn't.

A: You did. You're always doing things like that. I don't like you!

Get the children into pairs. Label the two children A and B. Tell the children that you are going to give each pair a 'concertina'. The pair is to read the scenario at the top of the strip and decide what happens next, that is, what the two friends say or sign. They can act it out in their pairs to give themselves ideas.

Give them two or three minutes to record their dialogue, helping individually where needed. They will probably need to work on tables.

Bring the children back around you.

Model acting out the scenario by going through the demonstration scenario with an assistant, including appropriate facial expression and body movement, as well as tone of voice.

Ask each pair to act out their scenario to the others. [This game is based on an original idea by WMQPEP.]

Process   Draw the children back around you and the flipchart.

Turn the concertina upside down and show how it is like steps which go up and up to end a friendship. Show them the new flipchart paper with 'broken friendship steps' on it. Ask the children how they feel at the beginning of the argument. How do feel halfway up? How do they feel at the end? Draw a diagonal arrow going upwards above the steps in red showing feelings, probably anger, growing and growing. Entitle the drawing 'Broken friendship chart' and keep it for the next session.

Mistake or not?

Deaf children (as well as normally hearing children) sometimes confuse something that was a genuine mistake for something planned.

Show the children one of the *'Concertina consequence scenarios'* or one of your own (which may be drawn from the children's own experience). Ask them if it could have been an accident or mistake, or perhaps there was a reason for it happening.

Give each pair a set of all the scenarios and ask them to put them in two piles 'Mistake' on the left and 'Not a mistake' on the right and 'Not sure' in the middle.

Give them three or four minutes to discuss together which pile they are going to put each scenario in. Individuals may not agree.

Write 'Mistake' and 'Not a mistake' and 'Not sure' on the flipchart and have some small pieces of Blu Tack Ready.

Draw the children back around you.

Ask one pair to bring you their sorted scenarios. Stick them under the columns that pair has suggested. Invite discussion from the other children. Maybe something happened through a misunderstanding or a miscommunication. Maybe there was a reason for what happened. Try to show the children that sometimes things are not what they seem. Discuss with the children what to do if something is just an 'accident' or misunderstanding, for example, 'Just say "sorry" and that's the end.'

End activity

Human knot

Everyone stands in a circle and raises their right hand in the air. Each player takes the hand of someone opposite them in the circle, not next to themselves. Everyone raises their left hand in the air. They take the hand of someone further away from them in the circle. Now the idea is to unravel themselves! It may take a couple of goes.

Consequence concertina scenarios

B tripped up A in the corridor.

A let B play with her toy. B wouldn't give it back.

B knocked off A's cochlear implant coil in the playground.

B pushed into the queue in front of A.

B wouldn't share the ball on the playground and A wanted it.

B cheated in a game and A lost the game.

B laughed at A's new hearing aids.

B tipped paint all over A's picture.

A knocked over B's drink at lunchtime.

A borrowed B's skipping rope and took it home with her.

Using Drama to Teach Personal, Social and Emotional Skills, Paul Chapman Publishing, A Lucky Duck Book ©
Jacqui O'Hanlon and Angie Wootten, 2007.

Session 3: Exploring Anger and Choosing

Objectives

- To continue exploring how feelings escalate and friendships break.
- To consider the idea of choosing whether to act out of anger or not.

Materials and preparation

- (For the activity *'I feel angry'*.) Prepare a flipchart sheet with a scenario on so that it is now in the 'first person', for example, 'He laughed at my new hearing aids'. (Choose your own scenario, either from those printed at the end of Session 2 or one which you know will be significant to the children.) The layout should be as shown below:

```
┌─────────────────────────────────────────────────────────────┐
│              He laughed at my new hearing aids               │
│                                                              │
│   I feel                                                     │
│                                                              │
│   Our friendship breaks              We stay friends         │
│                                                              │
└─────────────────────────────────────────────────────────────┘
```

- Use *'Human body'* from the CD-ROM. Produce enough for one for each pair of children (for use with *'Body drawing'*).
- Coloured pencils and ordinary pencils (for use with *'Body drawing'*).
- 'Broken friendship chart' from Session 3 (*'Consequence concertinas'*) (for *'Steps to friendship breakdown'*).
- Pan with cold water very near to the brim (for *'Steps to friendship breakdown'*).
- Flipchart and pens (for use with *'I feel angry'*).
- Blue curvy paper label with 'We stay friends' for use on the floor (for *'Steps to friendship breakdown'* and *'Conscience alley'*).
- Red spiky paper label with 'Our friendship breaks' for use on the floor (for *'Steps to friendship breakdown'* and *'Conscience alley'*).
- This preparation is for the activity *'Conscience alley'*. It is an additional and more advanced activity. Look at the description of *'Conscience alley'* and consider whether it is appropriate for the children you teach before embarking on this preparation.
- Prepare another demonstration flipchart sheet as follows. (Choose your own scenario, either from those printed at the end of Session 2 or one which you know will be significant to the children):

> He laughed at my new hearing aids
>
> Reasons why I should   Reasons why I should not take
>   take action   action
>
> End the friendship   Keep the friendship

Introductory name game

'What makes me angry'

Get the children to sit in a circle. Ask them to think about things which really make them cross or angry. This time tell the children that they can have their go in any order (because some children may need more thinking time than others). Start the children off with, for example: 'I'm Mr Taylor. I get angry when the traffic light goes red when I am in a hurry'. Whoever is next tells the group, 'I'm Sunita. I get mad when my friend won't let me have a go on the computer'. Ask an assistant to 'scribe' these different ways everyone gets angry on the flipchart. Ask the children 'who said/signed what afterwards' (to make sure they are attending to each other).

Core activities

I feel angry

Reveal the prepared flipchart as described in the 'Materials and preparation' section. Ask two children to come and take the part of friends. If you have chosen the example, 'He laughed at my new hearing aids', get one child to act this out. He might be pointing and laughing and saying the hearing aids look stupid, for example. Ask the other child to react with face and body to what's been said. Ask this child how she feels. Record mad, angry or cross on the flipchart beside 'I feel' and discuss how these words can mean the same thing. Ask the children what will happen to the friendship if the friend stays angry. Draw an arrow to 'Our friendship breaks'.

Body drawing

Get the children into pairs. Give each pair an A4 sheet with the drawing of the human body. Ask the children to imagine themselves getting angry (perhaps by thinking about the last scenario described above. They can act it out in their pairs to see how it feels). Ask them to discuss together, colour in on the picture and write in any words to show what happens to their bodies when they get angry. You might prompt them with 'Do any

72

parts of your body get hot?' 'What colour are you going to use to show you getting hot?' They may need to move away to tables for this but then bring the children back and display the pictures to the rest of the group and discuss them. [This game is based on an original idea by WMQPEP.]

Steps to friendship breakdown
By now it should have emerged that when we get angry we get hot. That is why the arrow on the 'Broken friendship' chart from the previous session is red. Show them this chart again. Show the children the pan with the water that is very close to the brim. Ask them what would happen if it were heated. Elicit that it would bubble up and spill over and hurt everyone around it. That is like us when we get angry. We bubble up and spill over and spoil our friendships. However, we don't have to. We can cool down. If we want to save our friendship we need to 'cool down'. Show the children the two floor labels – the red spiky one with 'Our friendship breaks' written on it and the blue curvy one with 'We stay friends' written on it.

Remind them of the connections – red and spiky goes with hot and angry. Blue and curvy goes with keeping cool and calm.

Tell them that one person is going to go out of the room. Meanwhile the others are going to place the two labels in two different parts of the room where they cannot immediately be seen. When the person comes in he or she takes one step. If the person is stepping towards the red label the group shout or sign urgently 'hot, hot'. If the person has stepped towards the blue label the group smile and call/sign happily and calmly 'cool, cool'. (Get the children to practise this with appropriate tone of voice and facial expression.) The aim is for the child to step towards the blue label and thus 'save the friendship'.

Have a couple of tries with different children going out each time.

Process   Gather the children together around you.
Discuss with the children what they have been learning through the game. They can stop getting angry and so stop breaking their friendships. They can stay cool and save or keep their friendships.

Optional activity

Conscience alley
This is an additional and more advanced activity that seeks to explore more deeply the causes of friendship break-up and the ability to decide between breaking up and staying friends.

Use the flipchart sheet described in the 'Materials and preparation' section. Ask the children for reasons why they might want to fight back or retaliate given whichever scenario is being presented to them; for example, 'People shouldn't treat you like that', and record under the 'Reasons why I should take action' column. Show the children that if they take action, their friendships are more likely to break up. Then ask them for suggestions as to why it might be better not to take action and record these ideas under the column 'Reasons why I should not take action'; for example, 'I'll get into trouble'. Ideas that you might wish to feed into this are: 'Did I really hear what he said properly?' and 'Maybe it was just a mistake'. Make sure that the children understand that in this case the friendship is more likely to remain.

Then nominate one child who is going to choose between the options and make a decision about which way the friendship will go. All the other children form a corridor facing one another. Each child looks at the flipchart sheet and chooses the statement that they are going to give – either to fuel the conflict or walk away from it. The chosen child starts to walk down, with you, as a facilitator, behind. You cue in each child by eye contact and each child makes their statement to the child walking slowly down the middle. When the child gets to the end ask him or her to pick up the suitable emblem of their choice – red spiky emblem ('our friendship breaks') or cool blue one ('we stay friends') depending on what he or she has decided from all the children's 'advice'.

Here is an example of how the statements might go:

Scenario:	He laughed at my new hearing aids
First child:	You should hit him because he deserves it.
Second child:	Don't hit him. You'll get into trouble.
Third child:	Hit him because he shouldn't get away with it.
Fourth child:	Don't hit him. It's not worth it. Just ask him why he laughed.
Fifth child:	Hit him. How would he like it if you talked to him like that?
Sixth child:	Don't hit him. Just tell him you don't like being laughed at.

If you have time, choose another scenario and consider the two columns – reasons to act and reasons not to act, again encouraging the children to keep their reasons to themselves this time rather than writing them down on the flipchart beforehand. Again the children should form a corridor facing each other while the chosen child walks down between them. On the eye contact of the facilitator, they come out with their 'advice' relating to the scenario as they see it. From this the one child makes his or her decision and chooses the emblem to denote the choice made.

Process   Tell the children that in this game they have started to see how we can make choices. We don't have to just 'go with our anger'. In the next session we are going to explore how we can 'turn the heat down on the pan' and cool our anger too.

End game

Mexican wave
Explain that you will start a movement that involves touching the floor and then standing with hands stretched in the air. You will then sit down. As soon as you are standing with hands in the air, the next person in the circle will touch the floor and continue the sequence around the circle. See how quickly the 'wave' can pass around the group.

Human body

Session 4: Practising Alternatives

Objectives

- To explore strategies for dealing with anger.
- To introduce the idea that one can think before acting.
- To introduce the idea that alternative choices can be made in difficult situations.
- To practise these alternatives.

Materials and preparation

- Flipchart and pens (for '*I feel calm when* . . . ' and '*Thinking and choosing*')
- Use '*Thinking and choosing*' from the CD-ROM. Make enough copies for one for each pair minus one because one pair will be acting the scene out and will not need a sheet.

Introductory name game

'I feel calm when . . . '

Get the children to sit in a circle. Ask them to think about things that make them feel calm. This time tell the children that they can have their go in any order (because some children may need more thinking time than others). Start the children off with, for example: 'I'm Mrs Singh. I feel calm when I watch the fish in my pond at home'. Whoever is next might tell the group, 'I'm Gary. I feel calm when I paint a picture' or 'watch TV' or 'stroke my dog'. Ask an assistant to 'scribe' these different aids to feeling calm on the flipchart. Ask the children 'who said/signed what afterwards' (to make sure they were paying attention to each other).

Core activities

Cooling down

Acknowledge to the children that it is an incredibly difficult to cool yourself down from being angry. But, there are ways to do this and that they are going to explore some of them in this session.

You have already collected some suggestions for things that make the children feel calm and these might prove a useful start for your next request. Ask the children what they would do to calm themselves down and record these suggestions in a list on the flipchart. You might get ideas like 'Breathe in and out', 'Go away and do something else' or 'Count up to ten'. Explain that soon they are going to try out some of the ways they've discussed but before that you are going to show them another strategy.

Relaxation exercise

Tell the children that it's impossible to stay angry when your body is relaxed. When we are angry we feel tense and our body is clenched but when we relax we can't feel angry any more.

Tell the children that in a minute they are going to lie on the floor and clench up their whole body. Practise this with the fist first. Make sure the children understand what you want them to do. Then you are going to ask them to relax everything. Again demonstrate with the fist and arm.

Ask the children to lie on the floor and clench everything. Go around checking tensed muscles. Then ask the children to relax. Check the floppiness of arms and legs.

Explain to the children that we can use relaxation as a way of calming down.

Thinking and choosing

The children will need to be in pairs at tables for this exercise. Give each pair a 'Thinking' and 'Choosing' sheet. Ask two children to perform the scenario up to the point of spilling the paint over the picture and then 'freeze'. Immediately each pair is to write down what they feel and what they think, imagining that it has just happened to them. Encourage the children to write exactly how they feel and think and not to worry about handwriting and spelling.

With these feelings and thoughts ask one of the children who has been writing what is the first thing he or she would say or sign to the child who has tipped the paint. How would this child reply, and so on until you have about five lines of dialogue. Ask the assistant to scribe this dialogue on the flipchart. Ask the original children who performed the scenario to act it out with full facial expression, tone of voice and upper body language.

Ask each pair to act it out.

Ask the children if this will end in 'Our friendship breaks' or 'We stay friends'. Agree that it will end in 'Our friendship breaks'.

However, tell the children it doesn't have to end like this. We have choices about how our conflicts can go. Challenge the children to think how it could end with 'We stay friends'.

Look back at the strategies on the flipchart for staying calm (first and second games of this session, *'I feel calm when . . . '* and *'Cooling down'*). What could they apply to this situation? Take suggestions from the group. Ask the original pair who performed the scenario earlier on to use one of the strategies, for example, turning round and going the other way, or counting to ten.

Ask the children in their pairs to think of another strategy that they could apply to this situation that would change its course to a more positive ending. Ask each pair to act out the scenario with their strategy for calming down within it.

Ideas for consolidation and transfer

If your group is more advanced or older you could consolidate this idea by returning to the *'Consequence concertinas'* of Session 2. Ask the children to write a new dialogue for this scenario along the steps of the concertina, taking into account the effect of a calming strategy, which will now **not** result in friendship breakdown. It might begin, 'I know you didn't mean to do it', 'I'm sorry'. Ask the pairs to act out the new dialogues.

You may wish to choose other scenarios from the end of Session 2 (or use your own), ask the children to act them out in pairs and, freezing, choose a calming strategy and carry it out and the outcome changing.

Ask the children to return to a circle. Ask them which calming down strategies they like and which they think they might use. Write each strategy as a column heading along the top of a chart and write the children's names down the side. In the coming weeks encourage the children to tell you when they have used one of the strategies to stop a friendship breaking, and reward with a sticker or house point on the chart.

End game

Circle mayhem

This is a game about making eye contact with someone else across the circle. In this game, eye contact is very important because once you've made eye contact with a person you swap places with them. You, as leader, take your chair out of the circle, once you have explained the game, so there will always be one person without a seat. That person can try to sit down when other people get up to swap places. Remind the group they can only swap places with one person when they have made eye contact with them.

Thinking and choosing

She tipped paint all over my picture

I feel

I think

Our friendship breaks   We stay friends

Module Five
'I'm Happy Being Me'

This five-session module has the object of increasing children's sense of self-esteem. This is a seen as a vital basis for achievement at school, and for sound emotional health in life. The module also prepares the children for the last module, 'I can express what I need', since it is from a position of feeling comfortable with oneself that one can be proactive about one's needs.

The content within this module develops through the introduction of a character, Jake, who may have some of the same feelings as the children. The children are able to focus on this individual to explore their own feelings and reactions to the factors within their lives. The main strategy promoted for developing happiness with oneself is positive self-talk.

A 'key facts' template for the character Jake has been included on the CD-ROM. Jake is presented as being a deaf child in a mainstream environment. Deafness is included among the factors in this child's life so that children can explore their own feelings about deafness through the character, if they are deaf themselves. Use this resource if it reflects the needs of the children you teach. Alternatively adapt the key facts for Jake and the other two characters to reflect the needs of the children you teach.

Session 1: Introducing Jake

Objectives

- To introduce the character of Jake and some facts about his life.
- To introduce two other characters, Deepa and Dan.
- To start to explore Jake's feelings about himself.
- To start to explore other people's feelings towards Jake.
- To start to encourage the children to help each other feel positive by expressing each other's strengths.

Materials and preparation

- Use 'Key facts about Jake' from the CD-ROM. Prepare enough for one for each child or copy the key facts onto a flipchart sheet if that is more appropriate for the children you teach. (For use with *'Introducing Jake'*.)
- Prepare one copy of 'Key facts about Deepa'(CD-ROM). (For use with *'Introducing Jake'*.)
- Prepare one copy of 'Key facts about Dan' (CD-ROM). (For use with *'Introducing Jake'*.)
- A large, long piece of paper. It needs to be big enough to draw a full-size child on. Wallpaper is ideal. (For *'Role on the wall'*.)
- Felt pens. (For *'Role on the wall'*.)
- Small pieces of paper and envelopes for each child plus pens/pencils. (For *'My secret key facts'*.)

Introductory name game – affirmation game

'Something I'm happy about'
Sit in a circle. Encourage the children to start thinking positively by focusing on one thing they are happy about – it might be the weather, a forthcoming birthday, a good piece of work they have done. Start off around the circle by telling the group, for example, 'I'm Mrs White and I'm happy because my cat has had kittens'. The next child says/signs, 'This is Mrs White. She's happy because her cat has had kittens. I'm Charlie. I'm happy because . . . ', and so on around the circle.

Core activities

Introducing Jake
Tell the children that they are going to 'meet' a new character who has a few problems. They are going to be working together to help sort out some of his problems.

Tell the children to move out into a semicircle shape so that they can all see what is going to happen.

Give all the children a copy of 'Key facts about Jake' or direct the children's attention to the key facts written on the flipchart.

Ask for a volunteer who is happy to read out loud to come out in front of the group and stand where everyone can see him or her. The volunteer reads the key facts.

Now ask the children to put down their sheets (if they have them) so that they are focusing on the visual image in front of them. The volunteer is now going to read the key facts again one by one. Engage the other group members in a discussion that seeks to make decisions about how to depict Jake in order to illustrate the kind of character he is. Keep the child who has read the key facts for Jake in front of the children in a pose that suggests his character.

Once Jake has been introduced tell the group that there are two other people to meet, Deepa and Dan who are important in Jake's life. Ask for two volunteers to come up and tell them about these characters by reading their key facts. These volunteers can then take up a still image in relation to Jake to show their relationship to him.

Process   Discuss with the children the issues that they think are facing Jake. Is he a happy boy? Does he have many friends? How does he feel about going to school? Immediately the children **may** start to make their comments in relation to Jake's deafness. It may become clear how they feel towards their own deafness – whether it is a cause of negative feelings or positive ones, or possibly some ambivalence. Allow the children time to voice their feelings, but don't, at this time, attempt to modify or influence their perceptions.

'Role on the wall'
Still in the large U shape, ask for a volunteer. This child lies down on the large piece of paper and you draw the outline of that child. Tell the children that this is now Jake. Give all the children a pen to write with. Ask them to write **inside** the body part of the drawing how they think Jake feels inside.

Then on the **outside** of the outline of the body, ask the children to write what other people think about Jake. You may need to prompt with questions. What do his teachers think about him? What do his classmates think? What does Deepa think of him? What does Dan think of him? What do his parents think, or his brothers and sisters?

Process   Read all the words that the children have written both inside and outside 'Jake'. Explain that they will be looking at that again in a following session. Also explain that they are going to carry on looking at Jake's life in the next session and seeing what a day in his life might be like.

Save the 'Role on the wall' sheet for Session 3.

My secret key facts

Give each child a small piece of paper and an envelope. Ask the children to look at the key facts for Jake again. Ask them to think about themselves and to write down three key facts about themselves on the secret piece of paper that they don't have to show to anyone if they don't want to. Give some examples, for example, 'I don't like writing' or 'I am good at swimming'. One or more of the key facts might be the same as Jake's. Ask the children to put their key facts in the envelope and to seal it and to put their names on the envelopes. Tell them they will be looking at them again in another session. The children may need to move away to tables to do this.

Hot-seating

There are four opportunities for hot-seating within these sessions. This means you will almost certainly need to 'hot-seat' more than one child per session to ensure that all the children have this experience.

Ask the children to come and sit in a semicircle if they have moved away. Tell the children that you are going to choose someone from the group to come and sit so that everyone can see them. That person will be someone who has done something really well recently (preferably during this session). Choose the person who takes their place as described.

Tell that person the thing that you have seen them do well and ask anyone else from the group to express something else they have seen this person do well. Write down all the comments that the children make. Tell them that you will be typing these comments into a certificate for the person to have next session.

End game

Stand, sit, wiggle, clap

Explain to the group that you are going to give them four instructions, to either stand, sit, wiggle or clap. Whichever word you say or sign, they must do the corresponding action. When the group is working well at this, explain that you are now going to change the rules! Now, all the words mean one of the other words – so when you say or sign 'stand', the group will sit; when you say or sign 'sit' the group will stand; when you say or sign 'wiggle' the group will clap; when you say or sign 'clap', the group will wiggle.

Key facts

Key facts about Jake

- He hides behind the dustbins at playtime.

- He thinks people don't like talking to him.

- He is good at football.

- He wears hearing aids.

- He draws very good pictures.

- His teacher thinks he works hard.

Key facts for Deepa

- She has just started going to Jake's school.

- She likes Jake's pictures.

- She doesn't like going to school.

- She helps Jake when he's not sure what to do.

Key facts for Dan

- He is in Jake's class at school.

- He is captain of the football team.

- He gets into trouble for talking too much in class.

- He is very popular with the other boys.

Using Drama to Teach Personal, Social and Emotional Skills, Paul Chapman Publishing, A Lucky Duck Book ©
Jacqui O'Hanlon and Angie Wootten, 2007.

Session 2: A Day in Jake's Life

Objectives

- To start to explore problems of the day associated with having a poor self-image, through the character of Jake.
- To give the children further opportunities to identify with Jake and so to explore their own feelings.
- To further encourage the children to help each other feel positive by expressing each other's strengths.

Materials and preparation

- On a flipchart write up different stages of the school day for Jake as a list, for example Jake arrives at school, a literacy lesson, playtime, an art lesson, lunchtime, going home time. (For use in 'A day in the life of Jake'.)
- A set of small cards for the game 'Wink murder' (from the CD-Rom). Cut enough for one card for each child (and staff).
- Camera. (For use in 'A day in the life of Jake'.)

Introductory name game

'Things I'm good at'
Have the children sit in a circle. Building on the last session where hot-seating was introduced, encourage them to start thinking positively about the things that are their strengths. It might be maths or PE but, equally, it might be tidying up, taking messages or looking after the hamster. Start off around the circle by saying or signing, for example, 'I'm Miss Parry and I'm good at remembering to send birthday cards to my friends'. The next child says/signs, 'I'm Raveena and I'm good at . . . ', and so on around the circle. (Unlike some of the other introductory name games it is advised that you don't ask the children to remember the contribution of the person who has preceded them. It will be enough for them to concentrate on their own honest contribution.)

Core activities

A day in the life of Jake
Explain to the group that today they will be bringing to life or acting out a typical day in Jake's life.

Using the headings on the flipchart, discuss with the group each stage in his school day. Ask for suggestions about what kinds of things might be happening to him and what he might be feeling at each stage. Include in your discussion suggestions as to what the other characters, Deepa and Dan, might be doing. Encourage lots of discussion at this point so that as many ideas as possible are generated.

Divide the group into new groups of four or five. Give each group a stage of the day, listed on the flipchart, around which to work. If the original group is small choose one or two stages of the day where Jake will have the greatest difficulty being himself.

Ask each group to create a still image of a moment in that stage of the day they have been given. To do this they need to discuss in their new small group what is happening in their moment. For example, if the group is creating a still image for 'A literacy lesson' is Jake being teased in class because he does not understand what he is supposed to do?

Ask the groups to show their still images one by one.

Now tell the groups that they are going to bring their still images to life. Tell them that in their scene each character can only speak once, so they need to think very carefully about what each character will say or sign in order to convey the meaning of the scene. Each group will need time to discuss what is going to be expressed and to practise it. For example, the group may have the still image title, 'A literacy lesson'. The teacher may say, 'I want you to write a poem'. Jake may say or sign, 'I don't know what to do'. Deepa may say or sign, 'You've got to write a poem'. Dan may say or sign, 'Why are you telling him things?'

Write down the expressions associated with each still image as these will be referred to again in Session 5. Also take photographs of the images for Session 5 (*A day in the life of Jake revisited*).

Process Ask the children again about the kind of life Jake has. Ask for their ideas about what he needs to do to be happier if, in their images, he does not appear to be happy. Again the issue of Jake's deafness may arise. For instance a child may offer, 'He doesn't like wearing hearing aids' or 'He doesn't want to be deaf'. Clearly such comments need to be handled sensitively, as they may well be a reflection of how the child expressing such things feels. However, the general aim is to lead the children to see Jake as having a wide range of traits that make up character he can feel good about – and likewise themselves.

Note: It may be that this exercise reveals deep and strong feelings that a particular child may have about his or her deafness (if you are teaching deaf children). This may provide an opportunity for a more sensitive exploration in a one-to-one session.

Save the flipchart sheet of stages of the day for Session 3.

Hot-seating

Give out the certificates from the first session, reading all the positive affirmations that were made. Ask the child or children to keep their certificates safely in their drawers (for Session 5). Now choose a new person to sit in the hot-seat and encourage the group members to express all the positive things that they have noticed about this person. Make a note of everything that is expressed and type it up for next time.

End game

Wink murder

Sit in a circle. Practise winking first! Hold the cards face down (keep the detective card out at first) and invite each child to take a card at random and not to reveal what is on their card. Tell the children that someone is the murderer and is going to try to 'kill' everyone in the group by winking at them. The children must look around at everyone and if they are 'winked at' they have to fold their arms and bow their heads because they are 'dead'.

Have one complete game and let the murderer 'kill' everyone if she can. Then play the game again, this time introducing the detective card. The child who gets this card is required to work out who the murderer is as soon as possible and stop that person 'killing' any more people.

Wink murder

Detective	**Murderer**

Session 3: Turning Negatives into Positives

Objectives

- To begin to turn 'negative self-talk' into 'positive self-talk'.
- To promote the skill of 'positive self-talk'.
- To explore the effect that 'positive self-talk' has on our mood and on our bodies.
- To further encourage the children to help each other feel positive by expressing each other's strengths.

Materials and preparation

- Flipchart sheet from Session 2 listing stages of Jake's day (for *'My Favourite Part of the School Day'*).
- 'Role on the wall' sheet from Session 1 (for *'Role on the wall revisited'*).
- Flipchart sheets and pens (for *'Role on the Wall revisited'*).
- Camera (optional) (for use with *'Self-talk statues'*).
- Two large baked bean or coffee tins (for *'Pass the Cans'*).

Introductory name game

'My favourite part of the school day'

Have the children sit round in a circle. Refer them to the flipchart sheet with stages of Jake's day written on it. Tell them you are going to start off around the circle by expressing what your favourite stage of the day is and why you like it. They are going to do the same. Ask the children to be as honest as they can. They may choose a stage from the flipchart or one of their own, for example, the PE lesson. If you are in a mainstream school you may like to encourage them to consider whether their favourite times in school are in the unit/resource base or in the integrated situation. Within the rules of the game, they are not allowed to choose a stage of the day outside the beginning and end of the school day. For example you may start with, 'I'm Miss Franklin. My favourite part of the day is science because I love doing experiments'. Continue around the circle. Again, children are not required to repeat the contribution of the person preceding them.

Core activities

Role on the wall revisited

Ask the children to widen out the circle to allow room to lay out the 'Role on the wall' paper. Remind them of this exercise and give them time to read through all the contributions they made, both inside and outside the body shape. Ask the children to be looking for all the **negative** things that Jake feels about himself and that may be going round his head during his day. Ask the children to 'call them out' and make a new flipchart sheet, writing these contributions up in (speech) bubble shapes in the first person singular, for example, 'lonely' becomes 'I feel lonely'. Take this flipchart sheet off and display it where all the children can easily see it. Then start another flipchart sheet and ask the children to begin to think about **positive** things Jake could say or sign to himself. This can be done in a number of ways:

- Look with the children at the things other people think about Jake that may be written on the outside of the body shape. For example, a teacher may think he's a really hard worker or his parents may be very proud of him. Ask the children to find ways of making these into positive statements. Jake can express to himself, for example, 'I try hard at school' or 'My parents love me' or 'I'm good at science'.
- Return to the key facts about Jake to find possible positive statements.
- They may like to reflect on how they feel about Jake, and why, and make these into positive statements, for example, 'People think I am good at scoring goals' or 'Deepa likes my dragon picture'.
- Turn negatives into positive statements, for example, 'I don't like literacy' but 'I like science'.

Record all these positive statements in (speech) bubble shapes on the second flipchart sheet.

Self-talk corridor
Ask for a volunteer to be 'Jake'. Tell the rest of the children that they are going to form a corridor that Jake is going to walk down. The corridor is a bit like Jake's head. The children are each going to say or sign the negative things that are in his head all day. (It may be useful to make a quick sketch here of speech bubbles inside someone's head to get over the idea.) Ask each person in the corridor to choose one negative thing that Jake might express to himself from the collection made on the first flipchart sheet. 'Jake' will walk down the corridor and each person will make one statement. Note that it is useful if the teacher or assistant walks behind the child being Jake and 'cues in' each person to make his or her comment.

(If you have a very small group of children it may be more effective for all the children to stand in a circle with 'Jake' standing. 'Jake' turns round and as he looks at a child, the child makes the statement. In this way 'Jake' can keep turning round and experience the same statements again until he is told to stop.)

At the end of the negative self-talk, ask 'Jake' how he feels. Comment if you noticed anything happen to Jake's body language as he walked down the corridor. Did his shoulders lower or hunch? Ask the children forming the corridor how they felt during the exercise.

Now repeat the exercise, but this time ask the group members to each choose a positive statement from the second flipchart sheet that Jake might express to himself. Ask 'Jake' to walk down the corridor taking in all of the positive comments. Again, ask him how he felt and comment on any differences you noticed in the way he walked. Also ask the other children how they felt.

Note: Always ensure you do the exercise this way round so that no one is left in a negative frame of mind!

Process Discuss with the children how telling ourselves positive things changes how we feel about ourselves and often how we look. Jake needs to tell himself positive things to make his days easier and happier.

Self-talk statues
Ask the group to create a group statue of how negative 'self-talk' makes us feel. Then ask them to make a group statue of how positive 'self-talk' makes us feel.

If you can, take photographs of these images to remind the children later how different negative and positive 'self-talk' makes us feel.

Hot-seating
Give out the certificate from the second session, reading all the positive affirmations that were expressed. Ask the child or children to keep their certificates safely in their drawers (for Session 5). Now choose a new person to sit in the hot-seat and encourage the group members to express the positive things that the group has noticed about this person. Make a note of everything that is said and type it up for next time.

End game

Pass the cans!
Have the children sit in a circle. Tell the children that they have to pass the two tin cans around the circle using only their feet. Set one can off in one direction and the other in the other direction. There will be an interesting moment when the two cans meet!

Session 4: Using Positive Self-Talk

Objectives

- To begin to demonstrate how positive 'self-talk' affects the way we think and behave.
- To further encourage the children to help each other feel positive by expressing each other's strengths.
- To demonstrate the uniqueness of each person in the group.

Materials and preparation

- Pieces of paper for each child. The paper should be large enough to draw their hands on. (For *'Handprints'*)
- Pens or pencils for each child. (For *'Handprints'*)
- An orange for every child (or potato). (For *'Oranges'*.)

Introductory name game

'Something I've done well this week'
Have the children sit in a circle. This game builds further on last session's name game by encouraging the children to think about achievements that contribute to them having a positive image of themselves. Tell the children that you would like them to think about something they have done well this week and start off with, for example, 'I'm Mrs Bright and something I've done well this week is to clean my house'. Continue around the circle. Again, children are not required to repeat the contribution of the person preceding them.

Core activities

Muscle testing
Ask the children to get into pairs. Label each member of the pair 'A' and 'B'. Tell 'A' members that they are going to think of a time when they failed at something or something didn't go well. Then they will stretch out their right or left arms (whichever is dominant). Their partners, the 'B' members, will try to push their arms down as the 'A' members relive their past disappointment. It should be very easy for 'B' members to push the arms down.

Now ask 'A' members to think of a time when something went really well and they felt really happy. Go through the same procedure of 'A' members extending their dominant arm and 'B' members trying to push their arms down. It should be much more difficult, if not impossible, this time.

Swap around the roles of 'A' members and 'B' members and try the same exercise again so that everyone has experienced the effect of positive and negative self-talk on their bodies.

Process   Ask the children if they were surprised by the exercise and what they think it means.

Handprints

Ask the children to form a circle again. Give out a piece of paper to each child and a pen or pencil. Ask each child to draw their own hand on a piece of paper. Ensure that each child writes their name at the top of the paper so it can be clearly seen. Tell the children that they will be leaving their paper with the handprints on their chairs. Everyone will have a pen and will walk around the room writing positive statements about each other in the fingers of each hand. So everyone will have five positive things written about them. Gather up the handprints before the children have had time to fully see their own. Keep them for the end of the next activity.

Oranges

Give each child an orange from bag. Ask them to study it very closely and so really become familiar with it. Then collect all the oranges and put them back in the bag. Then empty the bag onto a table. Each child must find their original orange. (Potatoes work equally well.) [This game is based on an original idea by WMQPEP.]

Process   Ask the children if they were surprised at being able to re-find their orange. We assume all oranges are the same and yet each one is unique. Ask the children how this might relate to the work we have been doing. Give out the 'hands' to the children again. Pass them round the circle so that everyone will read all the qualities that have been recognised among the group. Finally, let the children keep their own individual 'hands' and read to themselves what has been written.

Rolling images

Ask the children to get into groups of three or four. Each child will need his or her handprint. Now ask each child to decide on one comment they really like. Once everyone in the group has decided on one comment, they should, as a whole group, create a still image for each of the comments so that they have three or four images of the wonderful qualities contained in their group.

96

Ask each group to show its work and the rest of the children are asked to guess what kinds of qualities were being shown.

Hot-seating

Give out the certificate from the third session reading all the positive affirmations that were expressed. Ask the child or children to keep their certificates safely in their drawers (for Session 5). Now choose a new person to sit in the hot-seat and encourage the group members to express the positive things that the group has noticed about this person. Make a note of everything that is said and type it up for next time.

End game

Alphabetical order line

Tell the children that they are going to make a line based on the alphabetical order of their first names. Establish which way the line will go. The challenge is to make the line without speaking or signing. See how fast the children can assemble their line.

Session 5: Staying Positive

Objectives

- To give the group further opportunities to 'turn negatives into positives'.
- To encourage the children to 'own' key facts about themselves with which they feel positive.

Materials and preparation

- Flipchart and pens. (For *'One good thing about today'* and *'Never mind'* and *'A day in the life of Jake revisited'*.)
- Use the resource *'Never mind'* produced on card, if possible. Cut into individual cards. Label each card A on the back. (For use with *'Never mind'*.)
- Blank cards that are the same size as the cards described above as Card A. Have enough for 2 for each pair. Label each one B. (For use with *'Never Mind'*.)
- Blu Tac (For use with *'Never mind'*.)
- Photographs of still images and written expressions from *'A day in the life of Jake'*. Look through for one strong image which might be transformed with positive self-talk. (For use in *'A day in the life of Jake revisited'*. More details there.)
- Sheet of positive speech bubbles from *'Role on the wall revisited'* in Session 3.
- Children's envelopes with secret key facts in them.
- 'Hot-seat' certificates.
- Handprints.

Introductory name game

One good thing about today
Have the children sitting in a circle. Tell them that you would like them to think of one good thing about the day – it might be the weather, it might be something they're going to do later, it might be something about their lessons or about lunchtime or playtime. Start off with your own example, such as, 'I'm Mr Hart. One good thing about today is that Tejni made a lovely pot in Art'.

This might be a good time to record the children's contributions on a flipchart. By the end of the round you will have a number of positive statements that hopefully will make everyone feel positive about the day.

Core activities

Never mind

Tell the children something that could be perceived to be negative about your own day – maybe you were late getting out of bed, or it was raining, or the cat was sick.

Write up on the flipchart your negative event in a thought bubble, for example 'It's raining and cold this morning'. Ask the children whether they think it is a happy or miserable thought. Re-establish what it does to us when we have negative thoughts. Ask them how you could change it into a positive thought. You may like to produce a bubble that starts 'Never mind . . . ' so the present example might be, 'Never mind – I'll wear my warm coat and take my big stripy umbrella'.

Now read the two thought bubbles with suitable expression and body language. There should be a marked contrast.

Put the children in pairs. Give each pair a card with a negative statement from *'Never mind'* on the CD-ROM (labelled A). Also give them a blank card (labelled B). Tell them that you want them to think of a positive statement to go with their negative one and to write it on the card labelled B. Ask them to start the positive with card with 'Never mind . . . ' if that is appropriate language for the children. The children may need to work on tables.

When they have finished one pair of cards, give them another pair of cards labelled A and B and ask them to complete them.

Gather up all the cards. Spread all the cards labelled A face down in the centre. Spread all the cards labelled B face up on the other side of the room. Ask the children to come back to the circle of chairs if they have moved away to write. One by one ask each child to choose a card labelled A. (If a child chooses one that he or she has written ask them to choose again.) Ask them to go over to the B cards and to choose the B card which they think matches the statement on their A card.

Once you have checked that each child has chosen the correct 'partner' for their pair, ask one child to come and stick up his or her pair of cards on the flipchart with Blu Tack. Then ask the child to read the pair, starting with the negative card with suitable expression and body language. Go round all the children in this way.

Process   Ask the children how they felt when they read the positive card of the pair.

A day in the life of Jake revisited

You have chosen an example from the photographic images created from *A day in the life of Jake*' that it might be possible to change now that Jake has learnt about positive self-talk and turning negatives into positives. The original example in the text was: 'A literacy lesson'. The teacher was saying 'I want you to write a poem'. Jake was saying/signing, 'I don't know what to do'. Deepa said/signed, 'You've got to write a poem'. Dan said/signed, 'Why are you telling him things?' Broaden the circle of chairs into a semicircle with yourself at the head of it where everyone can see you.

Recall with the children the session when they created still images for 'A day in the life of Jake'. As it may have been rather a long time ago, show them the photograph of the still image you have chosen and the dialogue that went with it. Ask the original group to join you and to quickly show the rest of the group the image and to say or sign their character's sentence.

Ask everybody to concentrate on Jake. How is he feeling at this point? How can he change to feeling positive? What could he say or sign to himself? What could he do? Encourage the children to refer to the flipchart sheet with the positive speech bubbles. Encourage the children to think about the game they have just played, 'Never mind . . . '.

With respect to the image described in the text, hopefully the children will be able to volunteer Jake asking his teacher what to do or asking Deepa. Maybe he will tell Dan not to bother Deepa. He might tell Dan he doesn't care what he thinks and so on. Let the children act out the new version of the image.

Process   Discuss with the children how now Jake is happy with himself he can deal with situations better.

Hot-seating revisited

Hand out the final certificates for the children who were 'hot-seated' in Session 4 and carefully read out all the affirming comments. Ask the children who have already received certificates to get them ready for the next activity.

'My happy facts'

Ask the children to open their envelopes with the secret key facts in them and to have a look at them. Ask them how they feel about their facts. Give out their handprints. Ask them to read all the statements that people have said and written about them.

Ask them to change their key facts now to five that they are really happy with. They might like a completely new piece of paper and they might like to add to the ones they have already got.

Tell the children that this is going to be their special envelope of facts. They are not going to seal the envelope up again because now they are going to be able to look at them any time they don't feel happy with themselves.

On the front of the envelopes they might like to write 'Happy facts about me'. They might like to decorate their papers and the envelope.

Ask the children if any of them would like to read out their happy facts to the others. It would be very affirming for the children who feel they can do this. Let the children know that this is the end of the work relating to this topic, 'I'm happy being me'.

End game

'What I have learnt from these sessions about being happy'
Return to the circle. Round off the work by inviting each child to express one thing they have learnt from the sessions.

Never mind

A: My friend won't play with me.

A: I don't like my sandwiches today.

A: My dad's away working.

A: I had to stay in to finish my work.

A: I feel tired today.

A: One of my hearing aids is broken and I can't hear very well.

A: I don't know what to do in my writing.

A: I don't know what my friend said.

A: I don't like art and we are doing it this afternoon.

A: My mum was cross with me this morning.

A: Our dog is really poorly and I feel worried.

Using Drama to Teach Personal, Social and Emotional Skills, Paul Chapman Publishing, A Lucky Duck Book © Jacqui O'Hanlon and Angie Wootten, 2007.

Never mind

B

B

B

B

B

B

B

B

B

B

B

Module Six
'I Can Express What I Need'

This four-session strand is built on what has been learnt in the previous module, 'I'm happy being me', as it is from the basis of acceptance of self that a child can assert his or her needs. This module helps children explore elements of school life in a mainstream class that they feel are less than satisfactory, as far their needs as deaf children (or as children with other special needs) are concerned. It encourages them to identify solutions and to practise them. The content of this module is intended to move children away from passivity and into activity. It challenges them to move beyond feeling a 'victim of circumstances' and towards activity and change.

This forms a vital skill for children – both for school life and beyond.

If you are working with children with other special needs the content can easily be adapted to suit those needs.

To strengthen the effect of this work, let your mainstream colleagues know that the children are thinking about proactive solutions to difficulties that arise in class. Gain the co-operation of mainstream colleagues to allow and encourage the children to express their needs so that they gain confidence to solve their difficulties.

Session 1: Identifying Needs

Objectives

- To give the children an opportunity to explore the meaning of the word 'need' and how this relates to their lives in general.
- To start to explore how the children feel about being in a (mainstream) classroom.
- To start to express any difficulties they find about being in this environment.

Materials and preparation

- For the game 'Something I need . . . ' use 'Something I need' from the CD-ROM. You will need at least enough for one small card each. Cut up.
- Flipchart and pens (for use in 'Group discussion').
- Blown up balloon (for 'Pass a balloon around').

Introductory name game

'Something I need . . . '

Ask the children to seat themselves in a circle around a table. Spread the flashcards out while standing. Tell the children that they are going to choose one card and they are going to say or sign their name and then express what they need to do the activity represented on the card. Model this, for example, 'I'm Mr James and I need trunks and a towel to go swimming'. Continue around the circle in this way. Encourage the other children to think whether the child whose turn it is has forgotten anything that they need to complete the activity.

Tell the children that in this module they are going to be thinking about what they need and exploring how to express what they need to others. Tell them that first they are going to play a game about the things they need.

Mixing-up game

'All change if you need . . . '

Ask the children to move into a semicircle. Remove the table. You, without a chair, go to the head of the semicircle where you can be seen. Tell them you are going to say or sign something they might need and, if they need it, they are to stand up and change places with someone else.

Tell the children to be careful because they might not actually *need* the thing you are going to say or sign. Practise with an example such as 'All change if you need water' and 'All change if you need a new pair of shoes'. Remain the leader throughout and end with something everyone needs, for example, air.

Core activities

Classroom tableaux

This core activity is about re-creating a scene or scenes in the classroom where the children may experience different needs in relation to their hearing impairment, or other needs. Before the children are involved in this there is a 'warm up'.

Divide the children into working groups of between three and five and clear the space. Each group will create a still image of a situation you will give them, for example, a group of people at a fireworks display, on a fairground ride or on a beach.

Each group has ten seconds to work together to create the tableau you have chosen, with everyone in the groups taking part in the final image. Give a final countdown of 'five, four, three, two, one, freeze'. Comment briefly on what you see.

Now ask each group to create a picture of a teacher and the class. Give a countdown of 'five, four, three, two, one, freeze'.

Thought-tracking   In this part of the exercise you will start to get a picture from individual children about how they feel in a class situation. You will be sharing these experiences and feelings with all the other children.

Tap a child on the shoulder and ask them what is happening in the picture and how they feel. Continue around the tableau or tableaux asking questions depending on what you can see from the frozen action in the tableaux. Here are some examples:

Is the teacher telling anyone off?
What has happened?
Is this teacher a nice teacher?
What does he do that you don't like?
Do you know what to do?
Why is the teacher shouting?

Group discussion

Ask the children to rejoin you in a circle. Discuss with the children the kinds of things that happen in the classroom that they don't like. If you are working with deaf children your aim should be to elicit elements that relate to the children's hearing and their access to the curriculum and the life of the class. Draw out information from the children as you have observed it yourself in the classroom or recall problems which the children have formerly expressed to you, for example, again if you are working with deaf children, the teacher forgetting to switch on the radio aid transmitter, children not knowing what to do, the teacher drawing attention to the child by saying in front of the whole class, 'Can you hear me?' If you are working with visually impaired children it may be that the teacher has not enlarged the text. If you are working with children with communication difficulties it may be that something that the teacher said was not understood. Even if most of the children in the group have no significant special needs there will still be aspects of teaching within the classroom which children find difficult. It may be that they find it difficult to act on a series of instructions, for example.

Record the children's expressions on a flipchart. Acknowledge the children's contributions. Explain that in the next session they will be exploring how they can change some of these situations.

Keep the flipchart sheet for Session 2.

End game

Pass a balloon around

While the children are still seated tell them that in a moment they are going to stand up and form a circle standing up. You are going to pass the first child a balloon and the aim is to move the balloon all around the circle without using their hands. Discuss with the children the different parts of their body that they could use. Tell the children that if anyone drops the balloon they have to start again!

Something I need

Session 2: Creating Solutions

The material in this session is based around a problem which is pertinent to a deaf pupil. To give a sense of continuity the same example is used and developed in the following sessions. In this way a clear sequence is described which may be adapted for any child with a special need.

Objectives

- To encourage the children to be aspirational.
- To encourage the children to see that to fulfil our aspirations they need to take responsibility for their learning.
- To focus the attention of the group onto a specific instance of difficulty when learning in a mainstream class.
- To suggest solutions.
- To practise solutions.
- To identify the most effective solution.

Materials and preparation

- Use *'Don't just sit there . . . '* from the CD-ROM, or write some bubbles with other common problems that you know are relevant to the children. Cut them up. (For use with *'Don't just sit there'*.)
- Flipchart sheet from the last session listing areas of difficulty for the children in a mainstream classroom. (For use in *'One classroom tableau'*.)
- Camera. (For *'Photographic tray'* and *'Reframing the classroom tableau'*.)
- Flipchart sheet and pens. (For *'Photographic tray'*.)

Introductory name game

'Who I would like to be'
Sit in a circle. Remind the children that in the last module 'I'm Happy Being Me' (if you did that module) they spent a lot of time discussing all the things they were good at. Everyone has something to be proud of. There is something special about all of us. In this game the idea is to think who they know from the TV and history lessons that they would like to be! For instance, would they like to be another Florence Nightingale or a famous footballer? The children need to think about their response and why they would like to be the person they have chosen. Start off with yourself telling the group, for example, 'I am Mrs Wilson and I would like to be Lord Nelson because I love being on the sea and never get seasick

and I am a good leader'. Carry on around the circle with each child expressing who they would like to be.

Core activity

'Don't just sit there . . . '
Tell the children that if we want to achieve things in life we often have to make some effort for things to happen. We can't always expect other people to do things for us. Sometimes things go wrong and we have to sort them out.

The next game helps children to understand that they must take responsibility for creating solutions.

Divide the children into pairs and label each child in each pair A and B. Give each Child A one of the 'Don't just sit there . . . ' bubbles and allow them to read the bubble to themselves. Tell the children that Child A is going to read their bubble to Child B. Child B is going to respond with the question, 'What are you going to do about it?' The pair will discuss what they think will be the best solution and decide upon one. Then they should practise the whole dialogue. You may like to model an example with an assistant.

'I've lost my jumper.'
'What are you going to do about it?'
'I'm going to think where I took it off and go and look for it.'

When they have practised the first dialogue you will come round and give Child B a bubble and the children in the pair will swap roles.

Tell the children they have five minutes for this and then each pair will show their work to everyone else.

When each pair has shown both dialogues tell the children that they are going to use the same idea for solving problems in the next exercise.

Core activities

One classroom tableau
Have the children seated around you so that they can see the flipchart sheet from the last session on which is recorded the difficulties the children experience in the classroom as a result of their deafness or other special need. Read the contents of the list to the children. Tell them that

they are going to choose one of the issues to work on. Negotiate what this will be with the group. Make sure it is an issue they all identify with. The issue we have chosen for the purposes of describing the exercise and for following activities is:

The teacher writing on the board and talking at the same time.

Photographic tray

Inform the children that they are all going to make a frozen image of that problem as it happens in the class. Designate a corner of the room where the picture will develop in front of their eyes. The children will need to take the parts of the teacher, deaf children, perhaps hearing children and perhaps a supporting teaching assistant or teacher of the deaf. If no child chooses to take an adult part make sure that a teaching assistant takes the part of the mainstream teacher at least. Ask one child to take up a position to start the picture off. The other children will, one at a time, add into the picture until the group feels that it is fully developed. Ask them to think about the facial expressions and body language of the character they are going to play. Ask them to show how they feel.

Make the frozen image. When it is complete you could take a digital image, or a series of them.

You could 'thought-track' the children as in the first session. Tell them that when you tap them on the shoulder they will speak/sign to you as if they are the character they are playing. You could use prompts such as (to a deaf child):

'You look a bit sad, what's happened?'
'Why don't you say something?'
'Are you enjoying the lesson?'
'Do you know what the teacher wants you to do?'

Make sure you go to each child in the picture and ask different questions depending on how they look, for example, the hearing child may look bored with the lesson, or be messing about, or be getting on with their work. Be sure to also go to the teacher and ask questions such as:

'Why have you turned your back?'
'Don't you care about X who can't lip-read you now?'

(The answers the assistant gives in the role of the teacher can show that the teacher has just forgotten temporarily, in the flurry of thinking, about the rest of the class and getting through all the work. Stress that the teacher isn't being mean and may feel very, very bad that the deaf child could be feeling so isolated.)

Process Ask the children to sit back around you. Refer back to how the deaf child or children (when they were in role) express how they felt in that situation, and ask the rest of the group to express how they feel when they're in a similar situation. Acknowledge their difficulty, but tell them that now you are all going to change it.

Ask first if anyone has any good ideas about how they could solve that problem. For example, they might talk to the teacher about it after the lesson, or during it when the teacher comes round to help them. Discuss with them what they would say. Children who are shy may wish the teacher of the deaf or an assistant to say something to the teacher. Accept creative solutions, for example, making posters to go up in the school to show teachers and other staff helpful ways to communicate with deaf children. Stress to the children that the only 'solution' that is not acceptable is to do nothing! Note all these solutions on a flipchart and keep it for Session 3.

Reframing the classroom tableau
Divide the children into groups of between three to five children. Each group will take one of the suggested solutions and role-play it. Give each group up to five minutes to work on their solution. Each group begins from the starting point of the original picture of the problem. So, for instance, the teacher turns her back and continues talking. The deaf child says to the assistant sitting next to him, 'I can't lip-read the teacher.' The assistant asks the child what he would like to be done and so on.

See each group perform their solution. Take digital images of the children performing. Ask the audience for comments about what they enjoyed about what they had seen.

After seeing all of the groups, come back into the circle. Discuss with the children which solution they think worked best. Which one would they use? Why?

Once you and the group have agreed on which is the best solution, get the group who performed it to perform it again, as a way of affirming that choice. However, stress to the children that there are lots of different ways to solve problems and they can choose which best suits them.

If you have been able to secure the co-operation of mainstream staff, as suggested in the introduction to this strand, let the children know that the staff will be looking out for and encouraging the children practising their solutions to this problem in the classroom. Tell the children that in the next session they will be discussing any successes they've had in solving this problem, and maybe solve a new one!

End game

House numbers
Tell the children that you would like them to stand up and to get into a line in the order of their house numbers as quickly as possible. Nearest to you should be the lowest number and furthest away will be the highest house number. (If a child has not got a house number give that child an arbitrary number.) The children will need to communicate with each other. Challenge them to complete this game as fast as possible.

'Don't just sit there . . . '

Using Drama to Teach Personal, Social and Emotional Skills, Paul Chapman Publishing, A Lucky Duck Book © Jacqui O'Hanlon and Angie Wootten, 2007.

Session 3: More Solutions

Objectives

- To practise two vital elements to being proactive in this context – being brave and trusting others.
- To extend the range of issues requiring solutions.
- To explore solutions and identify the best.

Materials and preparation

- If you are with deaf children use *'More challenges',* from the CD-ROM, and cut it up. Alternatively use flipchart ideas from Session 1 that were generated by the children in the *'Group discussion'*.
- Large pieces of paper and pens (for use in *'More challenges'*).
- Glue sticks (for use in *'More challenges'*).

Introductory game

Something brave I'd like to do
Sit in a circle. In this game they are going to challenge themselves to tell the group something brave they would like to try and do. The 'brave thing' might be something they need to do to solve a situation in class or it might be something quite different. Start off with, for example, 'I am Mrs Jones and I would like to go up in a hot air balloon'. The next child says/signs, 'This is Mrs Jones. She would like to go up in a hot air balloon. I am Tejni and I would like to tell my teacher I would like to sit next to my friend in class'. Continue around the circle. Make a list as you are going along of all the brave things the children want to achieve and tell them that you would like them to tell you when they have achieved them so that the whole group can celebrate, perhaps even by the next session.

Core activities

Trust circle
Tell the children that they are going to play another game that is about being brave. This game works with groups of up to eight children. If you have more children than this you may have to play this game more than once.

Ask for a volunteer to stand. Ask the children to form a close circle around him or her, with their shoulders touching and their arms free to catch the child standing. Explain that the child standing will fall back into the arms of those standing in the circle and be passed around the circle. The child standing just needs to trust that he or she will be caught. He or she needs to stay on the spot and allow his or her upper body to be moved around the circle while his or her feet stay in contact with the floor.

After a short time bring the central child to a standing position and invite another volunteer to take the place of the first child.

Process   After the game has finished ask the children for their responses. How did it feel to be standing? What worries arose for them? What was it like to be part of the circle? Were there any concerns that arose being in that position?

Ask the children to recall what they did in the last session. Ask whether anyone has been able to change something that was a challenge to them in class. Tell the children that carrying out solutions sometimes means that they have to be brave and that they have to trust people. Remind the group that their teachers know about the children trying to solve their problems and are looking forward to seeing that happen. The children need to trust their teachers about this.

More challenges

Tell the group that in this session they are going to be considering other challenges in the classroom and solutions to those challenges.

If possible, divide the children into groups of three to five children. Tell the groups that they are going to randomly select one of the slips of paper with a 'challenge' on it. Each group is to be given a large piece of paper and pens. In the centre of the paper they should stick the challenge. Then all the children in the group are to 'Mindmap'™ different possible solutions to their challenge. Once they have done that they are going to discuss which is the best solution to the challenge. They are going to have about five minutes to do this.

Send the groups away to tables to complete this part of the task, and support the groups as appropriate.

After about five minutes ask for the children's attention. Tell them that after they have identified the best solution each group is to create a scenario showing their solution to the challenge. Ask the children to decide between themselves who will be the teacher, the deaf child, the assistant, other children in the class. When they show their work to the other groups they must make it clear what the challenge was in the first place. (They can do this either by introducing their work or by including the challenge within their work.) They have another five minutes to work out their scenarios.

When supporting the groups make sure that whoever is playing the teacher in the group reacts positively to whatever solution the deaf child brings to the situation. After five minutes, let the groups show their work to each other. Praise the groups for their work but keep discussion until all the groups have shown their work.

If there is time, the groups could try the whole process again with a second challenge.

Draw the groups back together. Discuss with the children what they have seen of each other's work. What did they think of the solutions brought to each challenge? Has anybody tried any of these solutions before? Which worked and which did not? Has anyone got an idea for solving something that happens in class from what they have seen?

Remind the children that there is always a specialist teacher or an assistant to help them to solve the challenges in class. They are not on their own.

Also remind the children that their teachers are waiting for them to put this work into practice. Tell them that you will be asking them in the next session whether they have had chance to create a solution to a challenge.

Note: Keep all the children's Mindmaps™ for the core activity '*A charter of advice*' in Session 4.

End game

Clap together
For this game the children need to be in a semicircle in front of you. Explain that you are going to clap your hands but that, as a whole group, they must clap with you at exactly the same time. Play with the time it takes you to bring your hands together – perhaps have a couple of false starts. You can then increase the speed of your clapping, turning it into a round of applause, and then decrease it suddenly to ensure the children stay focused.

More challenges

The teacher is always asking you, in front of the whole class, 'Can you hear me?'

The teacher sometimes forgets to turn the radio aid transmitter on when talking.

Children across the room answer questions quietly and the teacher does not repeat important answers.

The teacher separates you from your friend who is very helpful to you in class.

The teacher sometimes tells you off for not doing something, like lining up, when you didn't hear her.

The teacher often walks around the class so that you can't see his lips.

The teacher sometimes forgets to switch the transmitter off when she is not talking to you. You can hear her talking to other children, which is distracting.

The teacher gives instructions for the work but it's too hard to listen to her *and* remember them.

Using Drama to Teach Personal, Social and Emotional Skills, Paul Chapman Publishing, A Lucky Duck Book © Jacqui O'Hanlon and Angie Wootten, 2007.

Session 4: Advice for a New Child

Objectives

- To challenge the children to continue to be brave.
- To consolidate the work already achieved by creating a charter of advice for any new deaf child, or child with special need, coming into the school.
- To practise giving that advice to someone else and so affirm it for oneself.

Materials and preparation

- Flipchart and pens (for *'Charter of advice'*).
- Mindmaps™ from Session 3 (for *'Charter of advice'*).
- 'More challenges' from Session 3 (for *'Charter of advice'*).
- Art materials, a PC (for *'Charter of advice'*).
- Digital photographs from Session 2 (for *'Charter of advice'*).

Introductory game

Something brave that I've done

Have the children seated in a circle. If possible make sure that you have an assistant sitting on your right. Remind the children that in the last session they expressed all the brave things they would like to do, and that they started to solve their own problems. Tell the children that sometimes we have to be brave to solve problems. For instance if a child has left the radio aid in another teacher's classroom he or she might have to knock on the teacher's door when that teacher is teaching and ask for it back. The child might feel a bit scared but they still do it. That is being brave.

Tell the children that being brave is often a good thing and in this game you want them to think of brave things that they have done. They might have done brave things at school, at home or on holiday. Ask the assistant to lead off with an example, for instance, 'I am Miss Mistry and I rescued a spider from the bath and put it outside even though I don't like spiders'. As you are the next person, give the assistant a short round of applause and say or sign 'Well done, Miss Mistry' and then continue with your own example of bravery. Continue all around the circle. Encourage the children to applaud each other's expressions of bravery to affirm the idea that bravery is to be encouraged (usually!).

Core activities

A charter of advice

In this example again we have used the example of a child with a hearing impairment. Clearly this could be adapted to any child with a special need, or for any new child coming into the school. All children need to know to be proactive about their needs.

Tell the children that in this last session they are going to use everything they have learned in this module. The way that they are going to do it is to pretend that there is a new child coming to the school who wears hearing aids. Their task is to create a 'charter of advice' for that child. The charter of advice will tell a new child what they will need to do and how to do it. Give the children some examples from what they have done already. For instance, one piece of advice might be:

> 'Put up your hand if you don't understand something.'
> 'Give the transmitter to the teacher, already switched on.'

The first task will be for the children to decide what should go on the charter. Stick their Mindmaps™ on the wall to give them further ideas. Encourage the children to walk around deciding what should be included. Further stimulate them by presenting them with the slips of paper with 'more challenges' on them that perhaps they did not have an opportunity to solve. Give the children a large piece of paper and a pen to jot down the advice that they are going to include. Support the group in its decision-making and in how the work is allocated to individuals.

Encourage the children to use information and communication technology (ICT) skills and artwork and digital images of their work to produce the charter. Each child could produce one sentence, decorated in their own style, to be stuck onto the charter. Alternatively, a number of children could be in charge of the artwork, two children in charge of the text, others in charge of selecting digital images.

It is best if just one charter of advice is produced, but if the group is too big for this then you may direct them to producing more than one.

Tell the children that you are going to stop them after twenty minutes but they will have more time later if they need it to complete their charters.

Circle of advice

When each child is well on the way to producing their own contribution to the charter tell the group to stop for a few moments.

Ask if someone will volunteer to be a 'new child'.

Ask that person to stand and all the other children and yourself and assistant(s) should create a large circle around that child. Each individual child is going to tell the new child the advice that they are producing to go on the charter. If you have not organised the task like that, each child might choose the same point that they think is very important to tell the 'new child'. Ask for someone to start and the new child should face the first child giving advice. Before the child gives their advice they should take one step in as though to meet the 'new child'. When the advice has been given that child should step back again to the original position. When it comes to your turn, or an assistant's turn, make sure that you include a very positive statement about the help that staff can give, for example,

'Your new teacher wants to help you so please tell her when you need help.'
'I am always here to help you with anything you need. Just ask me.'

End game

'Something I have learned from these sessions'
Keep the children in this final circle, encouraging the 'new child' to join it. Ask the children to tell you one thing each that they feel they have learned from the four sessions.

Encourage the children to continue solving the problems they encounter in class and to tell you when they have so that the whole group can celebrate.

Compendium of Games

This compendium of games includes all the games that are described in the book. The idea is that games may be 'swapped' for others if they are deemed to be unsuitable for the group you teach. The games are organised under the same headings, for example 'co-operative games', as they appear in the book so that a similar type of game may be substituted. It will be noticed that some games appear under more than one category. This is because those games fulfil more than one description, for example affirmation game and name game. In some cases a little preparation is needed to play the game. Details of preparation are included within the description of the game.

Introductory name games

Middle, left, right
The children should be sitting in a circle. Introduce a 'talking object' (when the child holds it they may talk or sign). The idea is to pass the object around the circle and each person to first of all introduce themselves and then the person on their left and right. Model this for the children by saying/signing, for example, 'I'm Mr Phillips, and this is Charlie and this is Ayesha'. [This game is based on an original idea by WMQPEP.]

Module One: Session 1
Name and something I like doing
Make sure that everyone is seated in a circle. Explain to the children that they will each say or sign their name and then do an action for something they like doing. Model this by saying/signing, for example, 'I'm Miss Butler and I like singing'. Make an action for 'singing', but don't say the word. The group will then say out loud what the action is. Then the next person in the circle will say, 'I'm Mrs Best and I like (mime/sign for walking)'. This will continue around the circle, with the group naming the action each time.

Process Ask the group whether they noticed anything in that game? It might be that they mention how people like different things or how hard they need to concentrate to remember other people's contributions.
Module One: Session 2

Name and feeling

Make sure the children are in a circle. In this game the idea is that each child will show how they are currently feeling. Model this by saying/signing, for example, 'I'm Mr Cunningham and I'm feeling (mime action)'. Continue around the circle in the same way. At the end of the round, ask the group what feelings they saw. There will probably be a range of feelings including sleepy, sad, happy and angry. **Module One: Session 3**

Name and action

Ask the children to sit in a circle. In this game each person in the circle says/signs their name and completes an action with hands, arms, legs or feet. Start off the game by saying/signing, for example, 'I'm Mrs Hickman' and then touching your head with both hands. The rest of the group repeats the person's name and action. Carry on around the circle in this way.

Process   Ask the group what they noticed during the game. Perhaps they noticed that everyone had very different actions, showing their individuality, or perhaps they chose similar actions, showing how much we are like each other. **Module Two: Session 1**

How are you feeling?

Pairs of children sit together around the circle. Label one member of the pair 'A', and the other 'B'. Model what the children are to do, with a learning assistant. Member 'A', the assistant, adopts a facial expression and upper body posture suggestive of a feeling. You, as 'B', introduce your partner, identifying their feeling, for example, 'This is Mrs X and she's feeling moody'. Ask the children to continue this pattern around the circle. (The pairs do not need to discuss beforehand what feeling they will be modelling.) Now swap over. 'A' partners become 'B' and vice versa. **Module Two: Session 2**

Sharks

Ask the children to form a standing circle. A player enters the circle and is the shark. She says aloud (or signs) the name of another member of the circle. As she swims towards them, that person becomes the shark and their place in the circle is taken by the old shark. The new shark says/signs the name of another member of the circle and swims towards them, etc. Gradually, introduce two or even three sharks into the 'pool' at the same time. **Module Two: Session 3**

Hobbies

First, get the children to think about their own hobby and what mime they will use to represent it. (Deaf signing children will use signs.)

Sit in a circle, ideally with an assistant to your left. Start off, for example with, 'I'm Miss Smith and I like . . . (do the mime/sign for swimming)'. The assistant to the left then says/signs, 'This is Miss Smith and she likes . . . (mime/sign). I'm Mrs Jackson and I like . . . (mime/sign)'. The next child to the left around the circle has to remember Mrs Jackson's hobby before she/he says or signs her own. Go all around the circle. [This game is based on an original idea by WMQPEP.] **Module Three: Session 1**

Remembering something about someone
Sit in a circle. Tell the children that you are going to go round the circle and that everyone is going to try to remember one thing about someone else which they learnt in the previous session. Start off: 'I'm Mrs Wright and I remember that Rachel had the same favourite colour as me which is green'. Continue around the circle. Note the smiles of children who have had something remembered about them and mention this to the children. Praise children who have remembered something about someone else. **Module Three: Session 2**

Sharing
Sit in a circle, ideally with an assistant to your left. Ask the children to try to remember something that they have shared with another person in the time since the last session. Tell them that they are going to find out what other children have been sharing by asking around the circle. Start off the process by saying/signing, for example: 'My name is Mr Lilley and yesterday I shared my crisps at playtime with another teacher'. The assistant in the circle says/signs, 'This is Mr Lilley. He shared his crisps with another teacher. I'm Mrs Peterson and I lent my pen to my daughter Daisy'. Go all around the circle and praise the children for sharing. **Module Three: Session 3**

'I'm a good friend'
Sit in a circle. Ask the group to think about all the work they have done so far on friendship. Encourage them to remember the skill practised in each session. Now ask each person to think of one thing that makes them a good friend. Tell them that you are going to go round the circle and the children are to say or sign one thing that makes them a good friend. Start by saying/signing, for example: 'My name is Miss Hickey and I'm a good friend because I remember things people tell me'. And so on around the circle. If a child cannot express anything about themselves encourage the child by pointing out a skill that you've noticed they possess, for example, 'You waited for Arran while he did up his coat in the cloakroom'. **Module Three: Session 4**

Affirming someone's friendship skills

Sit in a circle. Ask everyone to think about the child sitting on their left. They should think of some quality in this person that makes them a good friend. Each child should then start and complete the following statement around the circle. For example, say or sign, 'My name is Miss Johnson and this is Dimos. He is a good friend because he helped Marsha on the playground'. After this initial example, withdraw from the circle yourself so that the children are just concentrating on each other. Prompt them as necessary and ask for suggestions from other children if a child 'gets stuck'. Try to ensure that each child has had something positive attributed to them.

Process Come back into the circle yourself. Ask the children how it felt to have positive things said about them. Refer to specific examples.

Tell the children that they should enjoy being paid compliments (use vocabulary here to suit the children's language level). It helps us to feel good about ourselves and about the person who expressed it! Tell the children that taking care of other people's feelings is what the session is about. **Module Three: Session 5**

My best friend

Seat the children in a circle. Start by modelling a statement about your best friend, for example: 'I'm Mr Wright and my best friend is Paul'. The child to your left then says or signs, 'This is Mr Wright and his best friend is Paul. I'm Mandy and my best friend is Holly'. Continue around the circle, with each new child having to remember and make a statement about the friend of the person before them, before making a statement about themselves. **Module Four: Session 1**

Compliments

Get the children to sit in a circle. Tell them that they are going to play a game now where they think of one compliment about the person sitting on their left. Give some examples. Then start with yourself, for example, 'I'm Mrs Bates and I'm good at making marmalade. This is Ahmed and he's good at swimming'. Ahmed will say or sign, 'I'm Ahmed. I'm good at swimming. This is Sarah and she's good at taking the register to the office'. Go all around the circle, with each child repeating the information about themselves and adding a compliment about the person to their left. **Module Four: Session 2**

'What makes me angry'

Get the children to sit in a circle. Ask them to think about things which really make them cross/angry. This time tell the children that they can have their go in any order (because some children may need more thinking time than others). Start the children off with, for example 'I'm Mr Taylor. I get angry when the traffic light goes red when I am in a hurry'. Whoever is next tells the group, 'I'm Sunita. I get mad when my friend won't let me have a go on the computer'. Ask an assistant to 'scribe' these different ways everyone gets angry on the flipchart. Ask the children 'who said/signed what' afterwards (to make sure they are attending to each other). **Module Four: Session 3**

'I feel calm when . . . '

Get the children to sit in a circle. Ask them to think about things which make them feel calm. This time tell the children that they can have their go in any order (because some children may need more thinking time than others). Start the children off with, for example: 'I'm Mrs Singh. I feel calm when I watch the fish in my pond at home'. Whoever is next might tell the group, 'I'm Gary. I feel calm when I paint a picture' or 'watch TV' or 'stroke my dog'. Ask an assistant to 'scribe' these different aids to feeling calm on the flipchart. Ask the children 'who said/signed what' afterwards (to make sure they were paying attention to each other). **Module Four: Session 4**

'Something I'm happy about'

Have the children sit in a circle. Encourage them to start thinking positively by focusing on one thing they are happy about. It might be the weather, a forthcoming birthday, a good piece of work they have done. Start off around the circle by telling the group, for example, 'I'm Mrs White and I'm happy because my cat has had kittens'. The next child tells the group, 'This is Mrs White. She's happy because her cat has had kittens. I'm Charlie. I'm happy because . . . ' and so on around the circle. **Module Five: Session 1**

'Things I'm good at'

Have the children sit in a circle. Encourage them to start thinking positively about the things that are their strengths. It might be maths or PE but equally it might be tidying up, taking messages or looking after the hamster. Start off around the circle by telling the group, for example, 'I'm

Miss Parry and I'm good at remembering to send birthday cards to my friends'. The next child tells the group 'I'm Raveena and I'm good at . . . ' and so on around the circle. (Unlike some of the other introductory name games, it is advised that you don't ask the children to remember the contribution of the person who has preceded them. It will be enough for them to concentrate on their own honest contribution.) **Module Five: Session 2**

'My favourite part of the school day'
Have the children sit round in a circle. Refer them to the flipchart sheet with stages of Jake's day written on it. Tell them you are going to start off around the circle by telling the group what your favourite stage of the day is and why you like it. They are going to do the same. Ask the children to be as honest as they can. They may choose a stage from the flipchart or one of their own, for example the PE lesson. If you are in a mainstream school you may like to encourage them to consider whether their favourite times in school are in the unit/resource base or in the integrated situation. Within the rules of the game, they are not allowed to choose a stage of the day outside the beginning and end of the school day. For example you may start with, 'I'm Miss Franklin. My favourite part of the day is science because I love doing experiments'. Continue around the circle. Again, children are not required to repeat the contribution of the person preceding them. **Module Five: Session 3**

'Something I've done well this week'
Have the children sit in a circle. This game builds further on last session's name game by encouraging the children to think about achievements that contribute to them having a positive image of themselves. Tell the children that you would like them to think about something they have done well this week and start off with, for example, 'I'm Mrs Bright and something I've done well this week is to clean my house'. Continue around the circle. Again, children are not required to repeat the contribution of the person preceding them. **Module Five: Session 4**

'One good thing about today'
Have the children sitting in a circle. Tell them that you would like them to think of one good thing about the day – it might be the weather, it might be something they're going to do later, it might be something about their lessons or about lunchtime or playtime. Start off with your own example, for instance, 'I'm Mr Hart. One good thing about today is that Tejni made a lovely pot in art'.

This might be a good time to record the children's contributions on a flipchart. By the end of the round you will have a number of positive statements that hopefully will make everyone feel positive about the day. **Module Five: Session 5**

'Something I need . . . '

Materials and preparation   Make a set of flashcards (one for each member of the group) representing different activities in which the children are commonly engaged, for example, swimming, painting, eating lunch (see the details of the game below for more details). Use symbols or writing depending on the children's needs.

Ask the children to seat themselves in a circle around a table. Spread the flashcards out standing. Tell the children that they are going to choose one card and they are going to say or sign their name and then express what they need to do the activity represented on the card. Model this, for example, 'I'm Mr James and I need trunks and a towel to go swimming'. Continue around the circle in this way. Encourage the other children to think whether the child whose turn it is has forgotten anything that they need to complete the activity. **Module Six: Session 1**

'Who I would like to be'
Have everyone seated in a circle. In this game the idea is to think who they know from the TV and history lessons that they would like to be! For instance would they like to be another Florence Nightingale or a famous footballer? The children need to think about their response and why they would like to be the person they have chosen. Start off with yourself telling the group, for example, 'I am Mrs Wilson and I would like to be Lord Nelson because I love being on the sea and never get seasick and I am a good leader'. Carry on around the circle with each child expressing who they would like to be. **Module Six: Session 2**

Something brave I'd like to do
Seat the children in a circle. In this game they are going to challenge themselves to tell the group something brave they would like to try and do. The 'brave thing' might be something they need to do to solve a situation in class or it might be something quite different. Start off with, for example, 'I am Mrs Jones and I would like to go up in a hot air balloon'. The next child tells the group, 'This is Mrs Jones. She would like to go up in a hot air balloon. I am Tejni and I would like to tell my teacher

I would like to sit next to my friend in class'. Continue around the circle. Make a list as you are going along of all the brave things the children want to achieve and tell them that you would like them to tell you when they have achieved it so that the whole group can celebrate, perhaps even by the next session. **Module Six: Session 3**

Something brave that I've done

Have the children seated in a circle. If possible make sure that you are sitting to the left of an assistant. Tell the children that being brave is often a good thing and in this game you want them to think of brave things that they have done. They might have done brave things at school, at home or on holiday. Ask the assistant to lead off with an example, for instance, 'I am Miss Mistry and I rescued a spider from the bath and put it outside even though I don't like spiders'. As you are the next person, give the assistant a short round of applause and say or sign 'Well done, Miss Mistry' and then continue with your own example of bravery. Continue all around the circle. Encourage the children to applaud each other's expressions of bravery to affirm the idea that bravery is to be encouraged (usually!). **Module Six: Session 4**

Mixing-up games

Walking name call

Explain that in a moment you will turn your chair out of the circle, say/sign someone's name and walk towards him or her. They will then get up so you can sit in their chair. Then they will say/sign someone else's name and walk towards them and sit in their chair and so on around the circle until everyone's name has been called and everyone has moved seats. Each person can only be called once. Ask the group what signal they could use to show that someone has been called? (Arms folded, for example.) The last person calls the leader. Once a pattern has been established, repeat the identical pattern again, so everyone has to remember whose name they called and sit again in their seat. Repeat the same pattern two or three times each time speeding up the game. [This game is based on an original idea by WMQPEP.] **Module One: Session 1**

'The sun shines on . . . '

For this game the circle of chairs needs to widened to create a semicircle. Turn your chair out of the semicircle and stand in a position in front of the semicircle so that everyone can see you. The idea of this game is that everyone moves who falls into the category that you present. For example, say or sign, 'The sun shines on everyone who can ride a bike'.

All the children who can ride a bike then change places with one another and you find a place as well. The new person standing has to carry on the game with their own phrase starting with 'The sun shines on . . . '. **Module One: Session 1**

'How do you like your neighbour?'
Have the children sit in a semicircle. One child stands where he or she can be seen by all in the space. This child says/signs to someone sitting in the semicircle, for example, 'Rachel, how do you like your neighbour?' She says/signs 'Fine, but I'd like to change them for X and X'. She names two other people in the group. The two named people swap places with the two children sitting either side of Rachel, and the child standing up in the space tries to sit in one of the chairs as the children swap places thus leaving a different person in the space. The game starts again with the new standing person going to another child in the semicircle and saying/signing 'How do you like your neighbour?' and so on. **Module Two: Session 1; Module Three: Session 5**

Circle mayhem
This is a game about making eye contact with someone else across the circle. In this game, eye contact is very important because once you've made eye contact with a person you swap places with them. You, as leader, take your chair out of the circle, once you have explained the game so there will always be one person without a seat. That person can try to sit down when other people get up to swap places. Remind the group they can only swap places with one person when they have made eye contact with them. **Module Two: Session 3; Module Four: Session 4**

Spin the plate
A player comes into the middle of the circle and spins a plate on the floor. He or she calls out or signs a name of another member of the group who has to get to the plate and pick it up before it drops to the floor. If this new player succeeds then he or she spins the plate and calls out/signs another name . . . and so the game continues. To make it more complex, the player can call out two names and both players called have to try to beat each other to get to the plate first. [This game is based on an original idea by WMQPEP.] **Module One: Session 2; Module Four: Session 1**

All change
The children are in a semicircle. Call out/sign, for example, 'All change anyone who likes football'. At this all the children who like football must

change places. Choose elements that are either hobbies/favourites/likes or dislikes for future elements of this lesson. During one of the changes sit down yourself, therefore leaving a child as caller. Encourage the child to choose similar types of commonalities.

Make sure you are at last the 'caller' and shout/sign 'All change', allowing all the children to get up and change seats. **Module Three: Session 1**

'All change if you need . . .'
The children are in a semicircle. You, without a chair, go to the head of it. Tell them you are going to say or sign something they might need and, if they need it, they are to stand up and change places with someone else. Tell the children to be careful because they might not actually **need** the thing you are going to say or sign. Practise with an example such as 'All change if you need water' and 'All change if you need a new pair of shoes'. **Module Six: Session 1**

'I sit in the woods'
A circle of chairs is needed with one extra chair. Everyone sits in the circle. There will be two children on either side of the empty chair. On a prearranged signal from you, both children will try to sit on the empty chair. The first person to get there sits on the chair and says/signs 'I sit . . . '. The person who now has the empty chair next to them moves into it and says/signs 'in the woods'. A third person moves into the empty chair and tells the group 'and I choose X (name) to sit next to me'. The named person now moves into the seat next to their friend. At this the whole process begins again. The two children on either side of the empty chair try to sit on it first. The first one to succeed says/signs 'I sit' and so on as before. No leader is needed after the first signal from the teacher as the game leads itself – an empty chair is an invitation to move. The children will enjoy racing to get into the chair and need to be warned to be careful that no one is hurt. [This game is based on an original idea by WMQPEP.] **Module One: Session 3; Module Three: Session 2**

Co-operative games

Follow the leader (detective)
(Preface this game by playing 'Follow the leader', with yourself as the leader, and modelling different kinds of actions. Then ask the group how they could disguise who was leading the actions.)

Keep in a circle but in this game one child (the detective) leaves the room. In their absence a leader of movements is chosen. This leader starts doing actions that everyone else in the room copies, for example, tapping knees, clapping hands, stamping feet. The leader should change actions as often as possible to maintain interest. The child who has left the room is the detective and their task, on being invited back into the centre of the circle, is to identify who is leading all the actions. The group need to make it difficult for the detective to guess, for example, by choosing to look at someone else rather than the leader. **Module One: Session 2; Module Two: Session 2**

'I sit in the woods'
A circle of chairs is needed with one extra chair. Everyone sits in the circle. There will be two children on either side of the empty chair. On a prearranged signal from you both children will try to sit on the empty chair. The first person to get there sits on the chair and says/signs 'I sit . . . '. The person who now has the empty chair next to them moves into it and says/signs 'in the woods'. A third person moves into the empty chair and tells the group 'and I choose X (name) to sit next to me'. The named person now moves into the seat next to their friend. At this the whole process begins again. The two children on either side of the empty chair try to race to try to sit on it first. The first one to succeed says/signs 'I sit' and so on as before. No leader is needed after the first signal from the teacher as the game leads itself – an empty chair is an invitation to move. The children will enjoy racing to get into the chair and need to be warned to be careful that no one is hurt. This game is based on an original idea by WMQPEP. **Module One: Session 3**

Fruitbowl
Arrange the circle into a semicircle. Give everyone the name of a fruit, for example apple, orange, pear and banana. Sit at the head of the semicircle so that everyone can see you. Tell the group that you are going to call out a fruit and everyone who is that fruit must move and must swap places with another person who is that fruit. Practise this. Then turn your chair out of the semicircle. This time the person standing will call out a fruit and will try and sit on a chair as the others move, so leaving a new person standing to call out another fruit. If the person standing calls out 'Fruitbowl', everyone swaps seats. **Module Two: Session 2**

Pass the can
Get the children to form a seated circle. Use a large, empty baked beans can. (These can often be found in the school kitchen.) Explain that you are all going to help pass the tin can around the circle. However, no one can use their hands or arms to do this, only their feet and legs. Place the can on your foot and send it to the person on your left or right. The aim is for

it to get back to you without being dropped on the floor. **Module Two: Session 3; Module Three: Session 1**

Pass the cans!
Have the children sit in a circle. Tell the children that they have to pass the two tin cans around the circle using only their feet. Set one can off in one direction and the other in the other direction. There will be an interesting moment when the two cans meet! **Module Three: Session 4; Module Five: Session 3**

Fives
This time the players stand in a circle. The teacher starts and explains that they will count from one to five around the circle and the person who says/signs five has to sit down and is out of the game. Players can say or sign one or two numbers at a time. The game continues until there is only one person left standing. This person is declared the winner.

Note: If you have a very small group, including assistants, it may be necessary to increase the number from five to six, for example. This way the game lasts longer! [This game is based on an original idea by WMQPEP.] **Module Three: Session 2**

Co-operative fives
This is an advanced version of *'Fives'*. Have the children stand in a circle. With the group, elect two children that the group are now going to 'save'. These two children will be the final ones left standing at the end of the game. In order to do this, other children will have to 'sacrifice themselves' and say or sign 'five' on purpose to get themselves out in order to save the appropriate two. Remember that the children can say or sign one or two numbers.

Note: Again, adjust these numbers to suit the size of the group. The smaller the group the higher the number should be adjusted up from five. Also if it is a small group you may only wish to save one person. [This game is based on an original idea by WMQPEP.] **Module Three: Session 3**

Feelings and facial expressions
Keep the children sitting in a circle. Ask each child to think of a feeling. Encourage them to be very specific about the feeling and use the flipchart sheet/s from Session 2 to extend the range of possible feelings chosen. Child X will start by modelling their feeling using facial expression and

138

upper body language to the child on their left. This child names the feeling they are seeing and then models a new one to the person on their left and so one around the circle. **Module Three: Session 4**

Affirmation games

Name and something I like doing
Make sure that everyone is seated in a circle. Explain to the children that they will each say or sign their name and then do an action for something they like doing. Model this by saying, for example, 'I'm Miss Butler and I like singing'. Make an action for 'singing', but don't say the word. The group will then say out loud what the action is. Then the next person in the circle will say, 'I'm Mrs Best and I like (mime/sign for walking)'. This will continue around the circle, with the group naming the action each time.

Process Ask the group whether they noticed anything in that game? It might be that they mention how people like different things or how hard they need to concentrate to remember other people's contributions. **Module One: Session 1**

Name and action
Ask the children to sit in a circle. In this game each person in the circle says/signs their name and completes an action with hands, arms, legs or feet. Start off the game by telling the group, for example, 'I'm Mrs Hickman' and then touching your head with both hands. The rest of the group repeats the person's name and action. Carry on around the circle in this way. **Module One: Session 1**

Hobbies
The aim of this game is to encourage children to think about their hobbies, or things that they like doing, and to remember one hobby of someone else.

Have the children sit in a circle, ideally with an assistant to your left. Start off, for example with, 'I'm Miss Smith and I like . . . (do the mime/sign for swimming)'. The assistant to the left then says/signs 'This is Miss Smith and she likes . . . (mime/sign). I'm Mrs Jackson and I like . . . (mime/sign)'. The next child to the left around the circle has to remember Mrs Jackson's hobby before she or he says/signs her or his own. Go all around the circle. [This game is based on an original idea by WMQPEP.] **Module Three: Session 1**

Remembering something about someone
Have the children sit in a circle. Tell the children that you are going to go round the circle and that everyone is going to try to remember one thing

139

about someone else which they learnt in the previous session. Start off: 'I'm Mrs Wright and I remember that Rachel had the same favourite colour as me which is green'. Continue around the circle. Note the smiles of children who have had something remembered about them and mention this to the children. Praise children who have remembered something about someone else. **Module Three: Session 2**

Sharing

Have the children sit in a circle, ideally with an assistant to your left. Ask the children to try to remember something that they have shared with another person in the time since the last session. Tell the group that they are going to find out what other children have been sharing by asking around the circle. Start off the process by saying/signing, for example: 'My name is Mr Lilley and yesterday I shared my crisps at playtime with another teacher'. The assistant in the circle says/signs, 'This is Mr Lilley. He shared his crisps with another teacher. I'm Mrs Peterson and I lent my pen to my daughter Daisy'. Go all around the circle and praise the children for sharing. **Module Three: Session 3**

Affirming someone's friendship skills

Sit in a circle. Ask everyone to think about the child sitting on their left. They should think of some quality in this person that makes them a good friend. Each child should then voice and complete the following statement around the circle. For example, say or sign, 'My name is Miss Johnson and this is Dimos. He is a good friend because he helped Marsha on the playground'. After this initial example, withdraw from the circle yourself so that the children are just concentrating on each other. Prompt them as necessary and ask for suggestions from other children if a child 'gets stuck'. Try to ensure that each child has had something positive attributed to them. **Module Three: Session 5**

My best friend

Sit in a circle. Start by modelling a statement about your best friend, for example: 'I'm Mr Wright and my best friend is Paul'. The child to your left then tells the group, 'This is Mr Wright and his best friend is Paul. I'm Mandy and my best friend is Holly'. Continue around the circle, with each new child having to remember and make a statement about the friend of the person before them, before making a statement about themselves. **Module Four: Session 1**

Compliments

Get the children to sit in a circle. Tell them that they are going to play a game now where they think of one compliment about the person sitting on their left. Give some examples. Then start with yourself, for example, 'I'm Mrs Bates. This is Ahmed and he's good at swimming'. Ahmed will tell the group, 'I'm Ahmed. I'm good at swimming. This is Sarah and she's good at taking the registers to the office'. Go all around the circle, with each child repeating the information about themselves and adding a compliment about the person to their left. **Module Four: Session 2**

'Something I'm happy about'

Sit in a circle. Encourage everyone to start thinking positively by focusing on one thing they are happy about. It might be the weather, a forthcoming birthday, a good piece of work they have done. Start off around the circle by saying/signing, for example, 'I'm Mrs White and I'm happy because my cat has had kittens'. The next child says/signs, 'This is Mrs White. She's happy because her cat has had kittens. I'm Charlie. I'm happy because . . . ', and so on around the circle. **Module Five: Session 1**

Hot-seating

Tell the children that you are going to choose someone from the group to come and sit so that everyone can see them. That person will be someone who has done something really well recently (preferably during the session). Choose the person who takes their place as described.

Tell that person the thing that you have seen them do well and ask anyone else from the group to express something else they have seen this person do well. Write down all the comments that the children make. Tell them that you will be typing these comments into a certificate for the person to have next session. [This game is based on an original idea by WMQPEP.] **Module Five: Session 1**

Handprints

Give a piece of paper and a pen or pencil to each child. Ask each child to draw their own hand on a piece of paper. Ensure that each child writes their name at the top of the paper so it can be clearly seen. Tell the children that they will be leaving their paper with the handprints on their chairs. Everyone will have a pen and will walk around the room writing positive statements about each other in the fingers of each hand. So everyone will have five positive things written about them. **Module Five: Session 4**

Something brave that I've done

Have the children seated in a circle. If possible make sure that you are sitting to the left of an assistant. Tell the children that being brave is often a good thing and in this game you want them to think of brave things that they have done. They might have done brave things at school, at home or on holiday. Ask the assistant to lead off with an example, for instance, 'I am Miss Mistry and I rescued a spider from the bath and put it outside even though I don't like spiders'. As you are the next person, give the assistant a short round of applause and say or sign, 'Well done, Miss Mistry' and then continue with your own example of bravery. Continue all around the circle. Encourage the children to applaud each other's expressions of bravery to affirm the idea that bravery is to be encouraged (usually!). **Module Six: Session 4**

Something brave I'd like to do

Seat the children in a circle. In this game they are going to challenge themselves to tell the group something brave they would like to try and do. The 'brave thing' might be something they need to do to solve a situation in class or it might be something quite different. Start off with, for example, 'I am Mrs Jones and I would like to go up in a hot air balloon'. The next child says/signs, 'This is Mrs Jones. She would like to go up in a hot air balloon. I am Tejni and I would like to tell my teacher I would like to sit next to my friend in class'. Continue around the circle. Make a list as you are going along of all the brave things the children want to achieve and tell them that you would like them to tell you when they have achieved it so that the whole group can celebrate. **Module Six: Session 3**

End games and activities . . .

'Something I've enjoyed today . . .

Sit in a circle. Each person completes this sentence and passes around a talking object as they do so. **Module One: Session 1**

Group whoop

Explain that everyone will put the tips of their fingers on the floor and from that position will begin to rise up until they are standing with their hands stretched up high. As they rise up they will make a corresponding sound that grows as they grow until ending with a big whoop when they are standing with hands stretched up. It should go very quickly and only take a few seconds to do. **Module Two: Session 1; Module Three: Session 5**

Feelings and events

Sit in a circle. Choose a feeling that you can identify as one that the children experience on a regular basis. Ask them to communicate in the final round about what situations trigger that feeling in them. For example, 'I feel angry when . . . ' or 'I feel jealous when . . . '. **Module One: Session 3**

Pass the smile

Sit in a circle. Explain that everyone needs to have a very serious face to start playing this game! You the leader will then turn to the person next to you and smile at them, they then turn and pass the smile on to the person sitting next to them, and so on around the circle until everyone has smiled. **Module One: Session 3**

Mexican wave

The group is all seated in a circle. One person stands up with their hands in the air and quickly sits down. As soon as they sit down the person next to them stands up with their hands in the air . . . this is repeated all round the circle as quickly as possible. **Module One: Session 2; Module Four: Session 3**

Pass the squeeze

All the children need to sit close to each other in a circle and link hands. The leader sends a squeeze to his left or right and the squeeze is passed around the circle until it returns to the leader. **Module Two: Session 2**

Circle mayhem

This is a game about making eye contact with someone else across the circle. In this game, eye contact is very important because once you've made eye contact with a person, you swap places with them. You, as leader, take your chair out of the circle, once you have explained the game, so there will always be one person without a seat. That person can try to sit down when other people get up to swap places. Remind the group they can only swap places with one person when they have made eye contact with them. **Module Two: Session 3; Module Four: Session 4**

'Something I like about being in this group is . . . '

Invite each child to express something that they have enjoyed about being in the group and doing this drama. **Module Two: Session 3**

Pass the can

Get the children to form a seated circle. Use a large, empty baked beans can. Explain that you are all going to help pass the tin can around the circle. However, no one can use their hands or arms to do this, only their feet and legs. Place the can on your foot and send it to the person on your left or right. The aim is for it to get back to you without being dropped on the floor. **Module Two: Session 3; Module Three: Session 1**

Pass the cans!

Have the children sit in a circle. Tell the children that they have to pass the two tin cans around the circle using only their feet. Set one can off in one direction and the other in the other direction. There will be an interesting moment when the two cans meet! **Module Three: Session 4; Module Five: Session 3**

Wink murder

Materials and preparation   A set of small cards for the game 'Wink murder'. Cut enough for one for each child, plus one more, (and cards for the staff). They should all be blank except two: one should have the word 'murderer' on it and the other the word 'detective'.

Sit in a circle. Practise winking first! Hold the cards face down (keep the detective card out at first) and invite each child to take a card at random and not to reveal what is on their card. Tell the children that someone is the murderer and is going to try to 'kill' everyone in the group by winking at them. The children must look around at everyone and if they are 'winked at' they have to fold their arms and bow their heads because they are 'dead'.

Have one complete game and let the murderer 'kill' everyone if she can. Then play the game again, this time introducing the detective card. The child who gets this card is required to work out who the murderer is as soon as possible and stop that person 'killing' any more people. **Module Three: Session 3; Module Five: Session 2**

Spin the plate

A player comes into the middle of the circle and spins a plate on the floor. He or she calls out or signs a name of another member of the group who has to get to the plate and pick it up before it drops to the floor. If this new player succeeds then he or she spins the plate and calls or signs out another name . . . and so the game continues. To make it more complex, the player can call out two names and both players called have to try to beat each other to get to the plate first. **Module One: Session 2; Module Four: Session 1**

144

Human knot

Everyone stands in a circle and raises their right hand in the air. Each player takes the hand of someone opposite them in the circle, not next to themselves. Everyone raises their left hand in the air. They take the hand of someone further away from them in the circle. Now the idea is to unravel themselves! It may take a couple of goes. **Module Four: Session 2**

Stand, sit, wiggle, clap

Explain to the group that you are going to give them four instructions, to either: stand, sit, wiggle or clap. Whichever word you say or sign, they must do the corresponding action. When the group is working well at this, explain that you are now going to change the rules! Now, all the words mean one of the other words – so when you say or sign stand, the group will sit; when you say or sign sit the group will stand; when you say or sign wiggle the group will clap; when you say or sign the clap, the group will wiggle. **Module Five: Session 1**

Alphabetical order line

Tell the children that they are going to make a line based on the alphabetical order of their first names. Establish which way the line will go. The challenge is to make the line without speaking or signing. See how fast the children can assemble their line. **Module Five: Session 4**

'What I have learnt from these sessions about being happy'

Round off the work by inviting each child to express one thing they have learnt from the sessions about how to be happy. **Module Five: Session 5**

Pass a balloon around

Form a standing circle. You are going to pass the first child a balloon and the aim is to move the balloon all around the circle without using their hands. Discuss with the children the different parts of their body that they could use. Tell the children that if anyone drops the balloon they have to start again! **Module Six: Session 1**

House numbers

Tell the children that you would like them to stand up and to get into a line in the order of their house numbers as quickly as possible. Nearest to you should be the lowest number and furthest away will be the highest house number. (If a child has not got a house number give that child an arbitrary number.) The children will need to communicate with each other. Challenge them to complete this game as fast as possible. **Module Six: Session 2**

Clap together

For this game the children need to be in a semicircle in front of you. Explain that you are going to clap your hands, but that as a whole group, they must clap with you at exactly the same time. Play with the time it takes you to bring your hands together – perhaps have a couple of false starts. You can then increase the speed of your clapping, turning it into a round of applause, and then decrease it suddenly to ensure the children stay focused. **Module Six: Session 3**

Bibliography

Bat-Chava, Y. (1993) 'Antecedents of self-esteem in deaf people: a meta-analytic review', *Rehabilitation Psychology*, **38**: 221–34.

Cayton, H. (1981) 'The contribution of drama to the education of deaf children', *Journal of British Association of Teachers of the Deaf*, **5** (2): 49–54.

Clark, P. and Fulwood, L. (1994) 'Social-skills activities to use with hearing impaired children', *Journal of British Association of Teachers of the Deaf*, **18** (3): 86–94.

Department for Education and Employment and Qualifications and Curriculum Authority (DfEE/QCA) (1999) *The National Curriculum*. London: DfEE.

Department for Education and Employment (DfEE) (2006) *Social and Emotional Aspects of Learning*. London: DfEE.

Goleman, D. (1996) *Emotional Intelligence*. London: Bloomsbury.

Gregory, S. (1976) *The Deaf Child and his Family*. New York: Haltsted Press. (Republished as *Deaf Children and their Families*. Cambridge: Cambridge University Press.)

Johnson, L. and O'Neill, C. (eds) (1984) *Dorothy Heathcote Collected Writings on Education and Drama*. Evanston, IL: Northwestern University Press.

Luterman, D. (1987) *Deafness in the Family*. Boston, MA: College Hill Press.

Marschark, M. (1993) *Psychological Development of Deaf Children*. New York: Oxford University Press.

Moore, M., Dash, J. and Bristow, L. (1999) 'A social skills programme with primary-aged isolated hearing-aid users', *Deafness and Education International*, **1** (1): 10–24.

Moseley, J. (1993) *Turn your School Around*. Wisbech: Learning Development Aids.

Powers, S., Gregory, S., Lynas, W., McCracken, W., Watson, L., Boulton, A. and Harris, D. (1999) *A Review of Good Practice in Deaf Education*. London: RNID.

Seeley, A. and Camus, J. (1983) 'Developing an approach to drama with hearing impaired children', *Journal of British Association of Teachers of the Deaf*, **7** (2): 30–4.

Warnock, M. (1978) *Special Educational Needs: Report of the Warnock Committee Enquiry into the Education of Handicapped Children and Young People*. London: HMSO.

Webster, A. and Wood, D. (1989) *Children with Hearing Difficulties*. London: Cassell.

Further resources

If you would like to develop the work relating to conflict resolution, please contact:

WMQPEP (West Midlands Quaker Peace Education Project)
46 Parkway Road
Dudley
West Midlands
DY1 2QA
Tel: 01384 234113
Email: wmqpep@peacemakers.freeserve.co.uk
Website: www.peacemakers.org.uk

CD-ROM Contents

Assessment and evaluation sheets

Module 1
Getting into pairs (Session 1)
Feelings (Sessions 2 and 3)

Module 2
Feelings sculptures (Session 1)
Pictures (Session 2)
Feelings improvisation (Session 2)
I know how to respond (Session 3)

Module 3
Who is the same? (Session 1)
Remembering is important (Session 1)
Secrets scenarios (Session 3)
Wink murder (Session 3)
Feelings (Session 4)
Friendship bag (Session 5)

Module 4
Consequence concertina scenarios (Session 2)
Human body (Session 3)
Thinking and choosing (Session 4)

Module 5
Key facts (Session 1)
Wink murder (Session 2)
Never mind (Session 5)
Never mind (blanks) (Session 5)

Module 6
Something I need (Session 1)
Don't just sit there (Session 2)
More challenges (Session 3)